ETHICAL MARKETING

Leon Jay

27 Easy Ways To Exponentially Grow Your Profit & Social Impact

Copyright © 2021 by Leon Jay, EthicallyMAD Ltd.

All rights reserved.

Published by EM Publishing

FIRST EDITION 2021

No part of this publication may be reproduced, stored, shared, or transmitted in any way (physical or electronic) without prior written permission from the author.

1st ed.

ISBN-13: 9 798596 477559

Disclaimer

All information in this book is true and accurate to the author's knowledge. However, he may be wrong. None of this information is meant, nor should be taken, as legal advice or absolute truth.

The content is meant as inspiration and education only. If you choose to use any of the information, ideas, or suggestions in this book within your own business, you do so at your own risk. Neither the author nor EthicallyMAD Ltd will be held liable in any way.

For further information and support please visit:

www.EthicallyMAD.co.nz

Dedicated to everyone in business who fully comprehends, and tries their best to follow, the words of Potter Stewart;

"Ethics is knowing the difference between what you have a right to do and what is right to do."

Contents

The Big Picture 1
- Sustainable Growth..2
- Know Thy Metrics 9
- Chicken or the (Golden) Egg?...13

Quality Traffic 19
- Focus on the Target 20
- Better Ad Copy..28
- Educate 35
- Manage Your Campaigns Well...39
- Get Referrals 41
- Use Coupons 44
- Search Engine Optimization (SEO) 47
  - **Site Structure**..48
  - **Content** 50
  - **Backlinks** 53
- Google My Business (GMB)...55

Onsite Conversions 59
- Messaging 60
- Copywriting...62
- Offer an Insane Guarantee 67

Use Testimonials and Reviews 69

Usability 71

Design 75

Live Chat 77

Dedicated Landing Pages 79

Site Speed 82

Conversion Rate Optimisation 84

Better Decisions Through Metrics 88

Follow Up 91

Stalking Professionally 92

Email 93

Broadcast 94

Event 95

Autoresponders 96

Support 98

Transactional 99

Retargeting 100

Social Media 102

Increasing Revenue 105

Adding Upsells 106

Have A Subscription Option 108

Promote Partner Products 110

Decrease Customer Cost 112

Increase Your Price 114

Bonus Tips 117

Create A Quiz 118

Choose Your Platform Carefully 120

Take An Agile Approach 123

Always Be of Service 126

Get Professional 127

About the Author 131

The Big Picture

The Big Picture

Sustainable Growth

Without awareness, care and responsibility, power can do a lot of unintentional harm. Intentional harm, on the other hand, would demonstrate awareness, but also suggests you are most likely a sociopath. For the purposes of this book, I am going to assume you are not a sociopath. (If you are, please stop reading now, and return this book for a full refund!)

You are about to learn how to harness a great deal of power. But it is not without trepidation that I share this knowledge with you. I have seen many students use the following information in ways that, without meaning to, caused social and environmental harm.

However, I see many businesses that work to make the world a better place and desperately need this information. So here I find myself, writing yet another book (a process for which I have developed a love-hate relationship).

Before we get into marketing and growth strategies though, a brief word on sustainability…

Businesses exist for reasons other than just making their owners or shareholders wealthy. A shocking and controversial viewpoint for some, I know.

Unfortunately, many businesses only use money in and money out as their yardsticks to set and measure goals. Focusing on cashflow only can leave them blind to the impact and consequences of their business decisions—even those run by good, honest, well-meaning folk (such as yourself?).

Despite the cry of many environmental extremists, business is not innately bad. Those very extremists, who bemoan business as the root of all evil, rely on them for their day-to-day survival. Businesses provide food, clothing, shelter, transportation, education, and a whole lot more.

At its heart, a business is a service to its community. With global trade and the internet, these communities are often much bigger than in the past, but the principals of service and value should still apply.

Businesses have a responsibility to provide jobs, help keep local economies strong, and of course deliver quality products or services to its customers.

However, they also have a responsibility to protect the communities in which their employees and customers live, as well as to clean up any environmental damage that may be caused as a result of their doing business.

If we want to protect the planet for future generations (and perhaps even our own), as business owners, we must consider the social and environmental impact that our business has, and not make our living at the expense of other people's health or future.

The Big Picture

Intentionally or unintentionally, every business makes a difference. The question is simply 'what type of difference?'

It is only delusion or ignorance to believe that our business has no negative impact whatsoever—even if that negative impact is purely from the reliance on a destructive supply chain.

If your business has a net negative impact, the more you grow, the more damage you will cause. If it has a net positive impact, then the more customers you get, the better off the world will be.

Effective marketing will amplify the result either way.

Too many businesses give little to no thought regarding their social responsibility. Some think they are simply too small, and that social responsibility is akin to corporate responsibility, so it does not apply to them.

On the other hand, many social enterprises and organisations view marketing as unnecessary, or worse, the work of the devil. Yet it is marketing that will help scale the positive impact they are striving to achieve.

More than this, when done well, marketing is a powerful and effective form of education. And, with sufficient education, social change takes place.

Indeed, it already has...

Marketing is (in part) responsible for:

Ethical Marketing

- Huge consumer debt and stress as people buy what they're told they should want, but can't afford

- Epidemic rates of obesity as vast numbers of people choose processed foods over natural foods

- Millions of deaths and immeasurable suffering due to excessive alcohol consumption

- Air pollution, water pollution, increasing carbon levels, deforestation, the extinction of countless species etc., all in the name of delivering us stuff, much of which we don't need, or just throw away after using it once

All these issues (and many more) are largely a result of marketers 'educating' people to desire and buy products from businesses that have yet to grow up and take responsibility.

Unfortunately, this has caused many people to conclude that marketing is inherently evil, and to be a marketer, you must be one of Satan's little helpers (and only marginally more likeable than a lawyer). But this is like saying a knife is bad because people have used them to commit murder. Knives also save lives.

Marketing is just a set of tools used to communicate a message. That message can result in harm or positive social change.

Think of campaigns to encourage people to wear a seatbelt, stop smoking, or not to drink and drive. Over the years, these have saved millions of lives, all thanks to the power of marketing.

During the 80s in the UK, organic food was found only in health food stores and small farm shops. Then something happened...

Waitrose began to promote the concept of organics. Their marketing efforts paid off, leading to mainstream awareness and education, followed by increased consumption of organic foods.

I am not saying Waitrose are angels. Nor that they successfully converted an entire nation to eat organic. But they did help trigger a significant shift in public understanding and drive demand.

Perhaps one of the most significant results from these early promotions was the pressure on other supermarkets to follow suit. By the early 90s Tesco, the UK's largest supermarket, began to put its marketing might behind organics. This success of its campaigns resulted in many farms converting to organics to meet the new demand.

In recent years, Tesla has been driving an even more dramatic shift; the move from petrol and diesel cars to electric ones. While the transition is still underway, the outcome is virtually inevitable at this point.

Many countries already have deadlines to phase out fossil fuel-powered vehicles, and just about every car manufacturer has an electric option or are in the process of releasing one.

This would not have been possible without both an incredible product, and a lot of impressive marketing. Thanks, in part, to the power of Tesla's marketing, cities of the future will enjoy much cleaner air, and global carbon emissions will be significantly reduced.

Without marketing, a superior product would have remained virtually unknown, and a social shift to a cleaner future would not have happened.

As a socially responsible business, it is as much your responsibility to educate society as it is to deliver a product or service. It is imperative that you take marketing seriously. Imperative for your business's survival, imperative to change consumer behaviour for the better, and imperative to put pressure on your competition to step up and do the right thing.

Many businesses that are trying to help society have an important message. Unfortunately, they often assume others already know what it is, they are afraid they will be seen to be greenwashing, or they simply don't know how to share their message.

Never assume that others know what you know or think the way you think. No two people have the same knowledge or have identical beliefs.

Even if your audience thinks the same way as you, hearing your message will likely make them feel they have found a

The Big Picture

business that aligns with their values. This sense of connection increases the odds they will choose to do business with you and that they will tell others about you.

Just because many businesses are unethical, and use greenwashing to trick eco-conscious consumers, does not mean you should not shout about the good work you are doing. For a start, if marketing sustainability did not increase sales, then the fakers and conmen out there would not be doing it.

It is perhaps worth remembering that politicians typically reflect the dominant social values of their communities. If a politician is outnumbered in his or her beliefs around climate change, it is unlikely they will have much influence or stay in power for long.

With encouragement and support from businesses and a more educated population, politicians will begin to develop more socially aware policies that level the playing field for all businesses.

With that said, let's grow your business and drive social change for the better...

Know Thy Metrics

Most businesses want to grow, yet few are clear what that growth will look like and have no plan to achieve it. Those that do have a plan are often vague at best.

To create a clear plan, you need to decide which specific metrics you want to increase. Knowing this allows you to map out your metrics in a flow chart to clearly see how you will achieve this increase. It also allows you to track everything and ensure that what you are doing is indeed working.

So, which metrics to measure?

Almost every business wants to make more money. And, as a business, profit is one metric you should definitely be measuring. However, I encourage you to think much bigger than just the bottom line—measuring social impact should be equally important.

To be clear, that is not one or the other. Or even one over the other. Give equal attention to both. We will discuss the financial metrics in a moment (and how they apply to marketing in particular), but first let's consider your business's broader impact.

The environmental or social difference that a business makes can be measured by its Social Impact Metrics (SIMs). These metrics may include the number of jobs it provides, the number of trees it plants, the amount of waste it recycles, the amount of energy it uses, or the amount of CO2 it reduces or offsets, etc.

Sometimes these metrics are easy to monitor. For example, at EthicallyMAD, we plant one tree each month a client uses our Google Ads service. Simply increasing the number of clients increases one of our primary social impact metrics. We also offset 360% of our carbon footprint, and protect 1000m2 of rainforest per client per month—so these are two more metrics we measure that directly correlate to our revenue.

Direct energy usage is usually as easy as checking your power bill. Seeing total energy use will often require digging a bit deeper. For example, your website servers, the email you send, the fuel used by staff getting to and from work, the equipment and raw materials your business may use—all increase your businesses total energy footprint.

These deeper levels can be difficult to quantify precisely in the same way as your power bill. However, becoming aware of them and then actively working to reduce them, offset them or eliminate them is not only the right thing to do, but may also provide you with a marketing advantage.

Take the Chia Sisters, a company manufacturing drinks in Nelson, New Zealand. To reduce their energy footprint, they converted their bottling plant to run off 100% solar power, a move which is now part of their marketing message. In addition to this, they invested in an EV, make careful choices regarding their supply chain, and have implemented a host of other changes to minimise their environmental impact.

These changes have helped gain them plenty of free publicity (and the right publicity can prove priceless as part of any good marketing strategy). It also provides material for their ads and social media that helps people care about them as a company.

Other times though, we may need to look at secondary SIMs to gauge how well a project is doing.

For example, if you have an international website that teaches people how to reduce power usage, monitoring its direct effect would be virtually impossible. Instead, you could look at other metrics, such as the number of people who visit your site, what percentage stay on your site, how often they return, the amount of time they spent on specific pages, and how much content is shared with others.

Each of these secondary SIMs collectively provides reliable indicators as to the effectiveness of your efforts to increase your primary social impact objectives.

As mentioned, financial metrics are just as important. Cash allows a business to operate and to grow. All too often, owners of social enterprises ignore the financial metrics in favour of focusing only on their SIMs. This can be a big mistake.

The Big Picture

The more people you reach, the more impact you make. If you are losing money on each transaction, then you won't stay in business for long. Goodbye positive social impact.

In essence, while profit is typically associated with capitalism, it is as necessary for running a social enterprise as it is for a greedy business owner or corrupt corporation. Don't feel bad about measuring and improving financial metrics or making money—just do so ethically!

Chicken or the (Golden) Egg?

Businesses typically fall into one of three types; those who spend a fortune on advertising and marketing, those with a modest budget, and those who won't spend a penny on it.

Guess which does the best?

There are exceptions to every rule, but more often than not, the big spenders will always outperform the others. The question is, do they spend big because they can afford to, or can they afford to because they spend big?

Well, a little of both, but there is another fundamental reason...

They can afford to spend a lot on marketing because they have learned how, on average, to make more than one dollar in profit for every dollar spent on advertising. Knowing this, they spend a lot, and so make much more in return. The more they make, the more they can reinvest. Therefore, they grow.

If I gave you two dollars for every one dollar you gave me, how many dollars would you give me? As many as possible! Good marketing and advertising will do exactly this (sometimes a bit less, sometimes a lot more). Yet most businesses stay small precisely because they are reluctant to spend much, if anything, on marketing or advertising.

The Big Picture

They see it as a gamble, or worse; just an expense that only the big boys can afford. This attitude has been the death of many a business.

The truth is, if you are getting less than one dollar back for every dollar you put in, then it is an expense. And, when you first run a new campaign, it is a gamble.

However, unlike most forms of gambling, once you have found the winning horse, you can keep placing bet after bet with a high degree of confidence it will continue to deliver results.

And, to put it bluntly, if you are afraid of losing money, you have no business being in business. Business is risky and comes with no guarantees. I have yet to meet a successful business owner who has not faced financial difficulty or loss along the way—and statistically, most businesses fail altogether.

Unfortunately, the vast majority of businesses, and even most marketing and advertising agencies, don't measure the return on investment (ROI) from their marketing budget; which is precisely why they need a budget. If they knew that something was making far more than it was costing, that budget would soon be made limitless.

There are only two times you need a fixed budget. The first is when you are testing new marketing ideas. This budget is the amount you can afford to lose if the latest ad or strategy does not work out (i.e., it makes less than it costs).

The second is when you are so busy you can't take on any more customers than you are currently getting.

For many businesses, there is no shortage of prospects waiting to become customers. The only question is, can you afford to acquire them? The chances are, you already have competition doing exactly that.

So, how can they afford to if you cannot?

A few answers to this question include existing market share, size of profit margins, and the ability to run their businesses more efficiently. However, there is one reason that usually trumps all other... conversions.

Many business owners have tried Google Ads, only to find they lose money. But does this mean that Google Ads don't work? Or could there be another explanation?

Given that $32.6 billion was spent on Google Ads in the last quarter of 2018 alone, you can be sure they work. While many large companies such as Hotels.com and GoDaddy spend millions every month on these Ads, according to WordStream, the average spend for a small business is between nine and ten thousand per month.

It is not that you need to spend this amount, or anywhere close to it. Plenty of businesses have a budget of just a few dollars a week. This is often because they feel they should be on Google Ads but can't afford to 'lose' more.

Businesses that measure and know their return can scale. If they cap at ten thousand dollars, it is only because that is

The Big Picture

the maximum amount of qualified clicks Google can deliver, or as much business as the business can manage.

There are several reasons so many businesses fail to make Google Ads effective. There is a lot to optimising a campaign; you need to choose the right keywords (and remove the wrong ones), you need to structure the campaigns correctly, write good ad copy, test your ad copy, and ensure a high quality-score on your site.

However, even with all of this done well, if your website fails to convert, you will still lose money.

It is not just Google Ads though. The same problem exists for all traffic—including leads from organic search, social media, affiliates, radio ads, newspaper ads, word of mouth referrals, and even your business cards.

When you look at the diagram below, it is not hard to see why. If your site fails a visitor by not providing the information they need or is challenging to use, they will be unlikely to become a customer.

Ethical Marketing

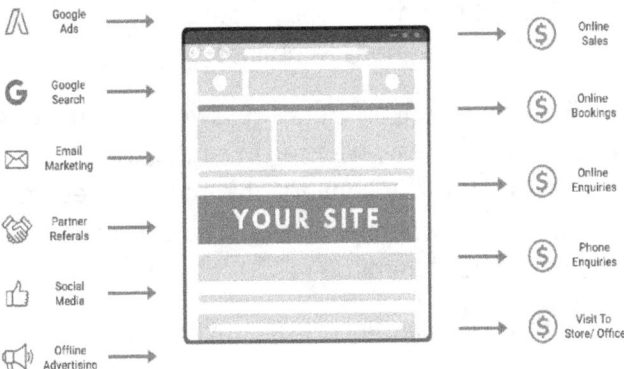

If you are looking for the 80/20 opportunity to grow your business, increasing conversions is probably it. Fix your conversions, and the results from everything else you do will improve.

No business can survive unless it can convert leads to sales. And the better it does, the more it can afford to spend acquiring those leads (and the less leads it will need to get the same amount of business).

The more you can afford to pay, the more customers you can buy. The more customers you have, the more profit you make. The more profit you have, the more customers you can buy…

Growth.

If your site does not convert, it does not matter how many people visit it; you will not make enough sales to survive. If your conversions are so bad that your site produces a

The Big Picture

negative ROI, the more money you spend trying to get customers, the more money you lose.

In AT LEAST nine out of ten sites we see, the easiest, cheapest, and fastest way a business can get more business, is to increase conversions. I always recommend addressing site conversions before considering any form of advertising or social media.

There are three ways to increase conversions:

1) Improve the quality of your traffic. This can be done by better targeting and by better preselling.

2) Onsite conversions. These can be improved by working on your messaging, copywriting, and usability, along with a few design tweaks.

3) Follow up. This includes email, retargeting, and phone, etc.

We will break down each of these and explore them in more detail in the coming chapters...

Quality Traffic

Focus on the Target

An archer does not just shoot arrows randomly. It is not that they would never hit the target; it's just that it would not happen that often. And, if they were relying on their shot to catch their dinner, they would go hungry most of the time.

The same is true of marketing.

Many business owners confidently tell me their marketing works because they are making sales. Yet when you look at how many arrows get fired, the sales are just a matter of statistical probability, not skill.

I have asked countless businesses, "Who is your ideal customer?" Yet few can give a focused answer. Most reply, "women over 25", "anyone who is sick", or worse; "anyone with money".

These are vague and generic. At best, they tell you roughly which direction to face, but not where to aim.

There are four reasons why people do not focus clearly... a lack of knowing better, a lack of time, laziness, or fear they will miss out on customers by being too narrow in their targeting.

Not knowing better will no longer be a valid excuse. Lack of time is a poor excuse, as it costs far more not to focus. Laziness is no excuse either, no explanation needed! But the fear...

There is a balance here. You want your focus to be narrow enough to hit the target with sufficient consistency, yet large enough you have sufficient business. However, for most businesses, consistency is the real issue. Unfortunately, they often mistake this for insufficient reach.

Take the time to define your perfect customer.

- Who needs or will benefit from what you have to offer, and has the means to pay for it?
- What age range are they?
- Which genders?
- Where do they live?
- What are their religious beliefs?
- Do they have children? If so, what age?
- Are they homeowners?
- What is their income bracket?
- What are their hobbies?
- Which websites do they visit?
- Where do they work?
- Where do they spend their time?
- What are their values as a person?

Quality Traffic

If your customers are businesses, it is still worth defining the type of individual who will be doing the purchasing. Remember, it is always a person that you will be selling to. In addition, you will need to define the type of business you are selling to...

- Which industries are they in?
- Where are they located?
- Which regions do they trade in?
- Which online services do they use?
- How many employees do they have?
- What are their objectives?
- What are their challenges?
- Who do they currently do business with?
- Who are their customers?
- What margins do they have?
- What is their annual revenue?
- What is their primary business model?
- Which industry publications do they get?
- What associations do they belong to?
- Which trade shows do they attend?

- Who in the business makes the decisions needed to purchase your product or service?

Once you have clarity, you can begin to do three essential things; identify where you might find your ideal clients, know how to filter those who don't meet your requirements, and know-how to communicate with those who do.

Even with traditional forms of advertising such as TV, radio, and newspapers, it is essential to make sure that you advertise to broadly the right population. There is no point in advertising as a local plumber in a local newspaper from a different region, or in advertising a retirement home on a radio station listened to mostly by those in their twenties.

One way to target in the offline world is to find specific places to advertise. For example, a power tool company may put their TV ads on during a DIY show, or print ads in a related trade journal or magazine (rather than a more generic newspaper or men's health magazine).

With the internet though, we can often target far more accurately—so long as you have identified who your ideal prospect is, of course!

Platforms such as Facebook have become trendy as places to advertise due to their ability to serve multimedia content, and for its ability to hyper-target your ads through demographic filtering. This combination of multimedia and hypertargeting makes for powerful advertising—assuming that your prospects are using Facebook.

(From an ethical perspective, many advertisers have chosen to boycott Facebook due to their privacy policies, and other ethical considerations. Ironically, it seems, most social networks appear to be doing more harm than good.)

If your targeted demographic is younger, you may need to focus on Instagram, YouTube, or Snapchat. The critical point to remember is to never fall in love with an advertising medium or platform (unless it makes sense).

Too many businesses and marketers focus on Facebook because of its sophisticated demographic profiling and the large numbers of users, without asking "are there better places to find my customers?"

This demographic profiling can be an excellent way to target prospects. There is, however, an even more powerful way—focusing on user intent.

As useful as profiling is, there are two glaring issues. Firstly, the majority of your targets, despite the profiling, will not be in the right space to act when you present your offer, or simply not want what you have. Secondly, many people will fall outside of your profiling who do.

This is where search engines come into their own.

If someone searches for "where to buy a 7KW home solar kit in Christchurch", and I sell 7KW solar kits in Christchurch, then I want them to find me. It does not matter what gender they are, their age is, whether they classify themselves as a film lover, or what their income is, etc. They want what I have, and chances are, they want it now.

With Google and Bing Ads, along with good SEO (Search Engine Optimization—i.e., getting found in the search listing without paying for advertising), you can target specific user intent within a narrow geographical region.

Targeting intent is marketing gold.

Even with search engine traffic, most searches do not identify the user's intent with such accuracy. For example, if someone in Christchurch is searching for 'Home Solar Kits', they may just be looking for reviews or other information. We cannot be sure they are looking for somewhere to buy one.

This is where a mixture of common sense and tracking is needed. To improve results, we first need to filter for negative keywords, then remove search terms that don't convert.

Negative keywords are words that identify someone searching is not our desired target. For example, someone selling exterior non-toxic house paint would filter out searches containing the words 'childrens', 'artists' or 'watercolour'.

As you can see, there are many ways to target a prospect. Targeting is rarely one hundred percent accurate, but it can dramatically improve our metrics. There are, however, some exceptions...

Quality Traffic

When Microsoft did a deal to supply its software on every IBM computer, it managed a virtually perfect score. It was so aligned and integrated, they did not even need to sell their software to the end customer.

While few products or services have the luxury of such integration into someone else's sales funnel, most can find ways to tap into similar opportunities. It just takes a little creative thinking, a bit of research, and some good negotiating.

As you can see, there is a wide range of possibilities and approaches when it comes to targeting, and each has its place. There is no definitive way you must do it; just be mindful of which strategy you are using, and why.

The purpose of targeting is to reduce your ad spend and increase your marketing's effectiveness to produce a positive ROI. If the cost of hypertargeting becomes so high you start losing money, or there are no longer sufficient customers, you will need to find other avenues.

On the other extreme, one of my clients had the worst targeting I have ever seen, and appalling conversion rates; yet the cost of advertising was so low, her return on investment was still a few hundred percent.

This was an exceptionally rare example, but it illustrates the importance of never losing sight of the end metric—ROI. While she could have significantly reduced her wasted ad spend, I'll take those numbers any day.

Look at where you are currently marketing, and how well you are applying filters to target your ads. Could you be doing better? Can you reduce wasted ad spend? Are you getting a desirable return on your marketing budget?

There is almost always room for improvement, and getting the best results usually requires ongoing refinement (especially for online paid advertising). When done right though, you will find the increased quality of traffic will increase your overall sales, and this almost always more than pays for the extra time needed.

Better Ad Copy

Getting your ad in front of your target audience is only the first part. Next, you must persuade the right people to take action (e.g., click on your ad, call you, visit your store or website, donate, etc.). Easier said than done, but doing so makes all the difference.

Usually, your ad will be alongside your competition's. If their ad has better copy than yours, they will likely get the business. You may know what you offer is better quality, better value, or better for the environment than the competition, but don't expect a potential customer to be a mind reader.

The challenge is to write an ad so good that the qualified prospects want to click, but the unqualified ones don't (so as not to waste money)—a delicate balance to master.

If you are using PPC (Pay Per Click, i.e., paying for each time someone clicks on one of your ads), you don't want to pay for leads that don't convert. If you are using CPM (paying a fixed rate for one thousand impressions), you would think the more clicks the better, but this is not always true.

If you are using Google Ads or Google natural search, you need to optimise your website's quality score—an unofficial score defined by Google's (ever-changing) algorithms.

Two important metrics that help define your site's quality score are the average length of time people spend on your site and the bounce rate (the number of people who leave your site without visiting another page or filling in a form).

If you are generating many low-quality leads that leave quickly without exploring the site or taking any action, then your quality score suffers. Should this happen, Google will penalize your site. And, if that happens, then your position in Googles search results will likely decrease, and you will pay more for clicks from Google Ads.

Contrary to what many people think, the amount you pay for each click in Google Ads is not fixed, nor is it as simple as 'the person who pays the most gets the top spot'. The amount you pay, and the position your ad appears in are defined by a variety of factors—the most important of which we will cover throughout this book.

So, how to write good ad copy?

An excellent place to start is at the beginning. In an ad, this is usually the headline. As one great copywriter once said, "the purpose of a headline is to get the reader to read the next line". While this may sound obvious, its implications are enormous, and often underestimated or ignored altogether.

If someone is not grabbed or engaged by the headline, then the probability is they are unlikely to read the rest of the ad (or page content, etc.). This means you lose the prospect before you even have a chance to start selling to them.

Quality Traffic

If you search a keyword for your industry, most ad headlines you will see are bland and generic—even those written by 'professionals'. Whatever you do, don't follow the herd. Instead, try to create a headline that grabs attention, makes it clear what you offer, and ideally evokes either desire or curiosity.

For example, at the time of writing, the current top result for 'Chiropractor Nelson' is:

> Tasman Bay Chiropractic - Primary Health Care
> [Ad] www.tasmanbaychiropractic.co.nz/ ▼ 03-544 4554
> Richmond Family **Chiropractor**, Primary Healthcare, Wellness. Call now!
> ♥ 64 Oxford St, Richmond, Nelson, Tasman District - Closed today · Hours ▼
>
> | Address | Contact Us |
> |---|---|
> | The Beginner's Guide To Chiropractic This Is The First | Contact Us For More Information. |

You can see that the top line is incredibly dull. The first three words are their business name. To put it bluntly, nobody cares about your business name. On the positive side, it does contain the word 'chiropractic', and the region.

The second three words, however, are much worse: Primary Health Care. This does not tell me anything and is a total waste of advertising space.

Instead, consider an alternative: Local Experienced Chiropractor | Get Pain Relief, Or It's Free

This ad gets to the heart of what someone is looking to find. They may be searching for a chiropractor, but what they are really looking for is pain relief.

Ethical Marketing

If they are searching, it means they probably don't have a trusted referral, so they need a way to choose between the different results. The word 'experienced' helps develop trust, but the guarantee of experiencing relief (or not paying) is enough to grab attention and build confidence.

The URL of your site shows next, and in this case, it's pretty good. The URL will not make or break your ad, but it can certainly help. Tasmanbaychiropractic.co.nz pretty much says what it does on the tin. There is little doubt that if I lived in Tasman Bay and was looking for a chiropractor, it would be worth my time to check this site.

Sometimes though, your domain name will sound unconnected to your industry. In this situation, there is a simple solution that can help. Take our own, for example...

EthicallyMAD.co.nz does not exactly shout that we are a digital marketing company. However, for an ad promoting our Google Ad services, we can display ethicallymad.co.nz/GoogleAds. Doing so informs anyone who sees the ad that the page they are going to is relevant to their search.

You can see the example ad for the chiropractor also includes their phone number, which is excellent. If you want people to call, make it easy for them!

Next, we come to the body of the ad copy, 'Richmond Family Chiropractor, Family Healthcare, Wellness. Call Now!'

Again, this is dull and only serves to repeat itself. Given the address and instruction 'Call Now' are displayed below, this line may as well not exist.

Remember, this ad displayed for the search Chiropractor Nelson, not Chiropractor Richmond (which is where they are located). The ad copy must speak directly to the search term. Doing this well requires writing many different ads to match the various search terms.

In this case, the ad displayed is not targeted well to the search. Richmond is 13.5km from Nelson, so it is not impossible to get clients who live between the two, but to do so, they would need more targeted copy and proper testing, as there are many chiropractors in Nelson itself.

Instead, consider:

We fix the cause, not just the symptom. No result, no fee. Call to book relief now.

This copy gets to the heart of people desires and concerns. They desire to be free of pain and for a permanent solution. They fear that it won't work, and they will just waste money.

Next are the address and opening hours. This is perfect, and something that their competitors who are also running Google Ads are not doing.

Under the primary ad copy are two ad extensions; Address and Contact Us. Unfortunately, the address section makes no sense at all. They are trying to get people to access a beginner's guide, but have put the call to action in the wrong extension type.

The result is confusion for anyone reading the ad, and confused people rarely act (at least not the way you want them to). Given that in this case, the search term was 'Chiropractor Nelson', we can assume the searcher understands the benefits of a chiropractor. So, in this case, they may be better off removing this section altogether.

In the final part of the ad, Contact Us, the phrase 'contact us' is repeated twice, simply wasting valuable ad space and wasting the reader's time. Instead, it could say:

Contact Us
to learn how we can help you,
or to book an appointment.

As you can see, every word needs to count, and each one designed to speak directly to the person searching. Essentially, your ad should aim to answer a few basic questions that your prospect is subconsciously asking:

1) What product or service are you offering?

2) How can you benefit me?

3) Where are you located?

4) Why are you better than the competition?

5) Why should I trust you?

The better you address these questions, the higher the probability of getting qualified leads to click on your ad

Quality Traffic

(rather than on the competition's). This is true for all ad types, as well as for the content of your website.

Educate

One of the most powerful yet underutilised aspects of marketing is its ability to educate. When a qualified prospect is adequately educated, there should be no need to sell. They come to you already wanting to buy.

Too much advertising is based on branding and not enough on education. Think about how many times you need to see branding to be influenced by it, versus learning useful, emotionally engaging, or interesting information. (Of course, robust education also helps build a brand.)

Many businesses rely on getting a prospect to their website, phone line, or store to begin the education process. But if advertising and premarketing are done well, leads come to these places because they already know what they want, and why they want it.

Not to say you don't continue the education process when someone arrives at your site or store. But if we educate leads from the first contact, we not only increase the number of people who visit, but the percentage who convert when they do.

If the advertising you are using has little space, focus on your core point of difference or key benefit. If you have more room, then make use of it.

Another advantage of educating prospects is the increased chance they will tell their friends. People love to be seen as knowledgeable. When you give them information that's interesting or useful, they are likely to share it.

Which leads us to marketing's most significant potential for any business that operates with purpose...

Creating social change.

If education is based on lies or misinformation, we call it propaganda. If it functions to manipulate people into buying stuff they don't need, we may call it brainwashing. But if that education leads to positive social impact, we can call it a movement or a force for improving society.

Whichever way you look at it, education can change the beliefs and behaviours of those exposed to it.

When you understand the true power of marketing as a medium to educate and the full potential of education, you start to glimpse the responsibility of wielding such power.

As we face so many social and environmental challenges, I am often asked what chance I think we have of changing political, corporate, and consumer behaviour in time to prevent the seemingly inevitable disaster ahead.

It's important to understand the reason we are in this mess to begin with. For a long time now, we have been taught to desire material wealth and success, but without being taught the consequences.

Business owners have been allowed to squander the world's resources for their personal gain. And, as consumers, we have financially supported this environmental destruction, as it has allowed us to experience greater degrees of comfort for less than the true cost.

Think of the environment like a bank account. If you can live on the interest only, it is sustainable. However, if constant withdrawals exceed the interest amount, the account becomes increasing low, until it goes into debt and, eventually, bankruptcy.

Businesses rely (directly or indirectly) on the ability to convert environmental resources into actual cash (fisheries, farming, oil and gas, mining, real estate, etc.). If this is done at a rate faster than these resources can replenish themselves, or the damage done is not repaired, we have an escalating problem.

Take, for example, the dairy industry—an especially sensitive subject here in New Zealand. Many dairy farms are polluting rivers, and do so because, with current milk prices, they find it economically challenging to prevent nitrates leaching into the waterways. The taxpayer then gets footed with the bill to clean the mess, or must live with the consequences.

This is madness. A product's real cost should be passed directly to the consumer, including the cost of protecting the environment.

If not, it is socially irresponsible, unfair to those who don't consume dairy and lacks consideration to the future generations that will have to pay the price to clean up our consumption today.

Yet, I am still optimistic about our future – for two key reasons; our ability to develop new technologies at an exponential rate, and the shift taking place in public awareness and expectation.

While marketing has driven much of today's excessive consumption that has led to the current crisis, it also offers a critical part of the solution.

Marketing social enterprises offer a win-win-win opportunity. By using the marketing budget to educate people, we can influence consumer behaviour for the better, move sales from an old school business to a socially responsible business, increase expectations on other companies to do the right thing, and help move society toward a better future for all.

Consider the outdoor brand Patagonia. Their marketing has educated consumers about the social and environmental damage being caused by supporting its industry. By offering solutions to these problems, many people now choose their products over the competitions.

In doing so, they have put pressure on competitors to improve their own social and environmental impact metrics. While there is still a long way to go (as even Patagonia themselves acknowledge), there is progress. And, it is marketing dollars that help drive this change in social attitudes.

Manage Your Campaigns Well

Many businesses setup ad campaigns with little time or thought and then expect them to do well. Others set them up well, only to then ignore them. This is especially true of Google Ad campaigns.

Most people don't do a proper job because they don't have time, they want to save a few bucks by doing it themselves, or they resent paying a professional. However, if your campaigns are not set up or managed well, you will pay a much higher price.

When ads are poorly managed, they generate a lot of low-quality leads that will never convert, no matter how good your website. This not only affects your overall site conversion rate, but also means you will generally pay more for your ads too. A double loss.

The bad news is that managing ad campaigns well takes skill and time. Just learning to do it well would take more than an entire book devoted to this topic alone. The good news is that getting a professional to do it not only saves you time but should give you a good return on investment too.

When campaigns are managed well, you decrease the cost you pay for each lead, and you increase the number of leads who convert to sales. An optimised campaign allow you to be more competitive, and so you can afford to reach more qualified leads, thus growing your business.

Quality Traffic

This reduction in costs, and an increase in sales, more than cover the cost of paying for someone who knows what they are doing. Add to the bottom line the saving of your time, which you can now use for growing your business in other ways, and you are way ahead.

Try to avoid the all-too-common mistake of delegating this task to your receptionist or unqualified employee. Yes, most people who know how to use a computer can set up an ad campaign—but there is no way they have the time, training, or experience to manage it well.

Simply put, you will lose far more than you think you are saving.

Some agencies (such as EthicallyMAD) are so confident that they will get you a good return, that they will only charge if they can improve what you already have. If not, you pay nothing (so there is zero risk in trying).

Get Referrals

Referrals are the holy grail of leads. They convert incredibly well, are known for being easier to deal with (on average) than prospects from other sources and are generally free.

Even so, most businesses don't bother to ask for them. With no active strategy in place to get such leads, they rely instead on pure chance. This is clearly crazy!

I understand, few people like asking for a referral, and it can be easy to forget to do. But so long as you can capture a customer's email address, neither are a good excuse. Simply set up an automated email to go out after a set period.

This email takes minutes to write, but once part of your post-sales process, it will keep working and generating new leads for you on complete autopilot. And not just any leads—the best-converting leads, and virtually for free.

If you don't have anything like this in place right now, you should be kicking yourself. You are literally losing customers that don't cost a cent in advertising. But, before you race off to set one up, let me share a few tips...

Many businesses make the mistake of trying to incentivise their customers to make a referral. Bribery can work but is often not the best strategy (incentivisation is essential for professional affiliates—but that's a topic for another chapter).

Quality Traffic

Psychological tests have shown, unsurprisingly, that most people don't like to feel they are profiting from their friends. Instead, they prefer to give something of value; paying it forward, so to speak. Think of it as a form of social currency.

By sending your customers a discount (20% off their first purchase), a special offer (get two meals for the price of one), or free gift (one hour of consulting) to give to their friends, they are far more likely to pass it on. It makes them look good and feel good.

Another form of social currency is useful information. This ties-in exceptionally well when you have a message of value to share.

For example, if you sell paint that is safe for babies, there is a higher probability that mothers will share this information with other mothers. To help them, you can create a short report to send a new customer covering the dangers of standard commercial paint and the differences of your safer paint.

Along with this report, make a simple request: "Please pass this on to anyone you know who has a baby and may find the information valuable. Together, we make a difference. Thanks in advance."

Giving people a reason to act, and requesting them to do so, dramatically increases your chances of a referral. And—the more meaningful, useful, and absorbing your message, the greater your referral success will be (few people want to pass on direct sales hype).

If you want to increase both the referral rate and the response rate of referrals, try combining both strategies: i.e., including an incentive for the person being referred within the great content.

Incentivisation could be as simple as including a coupon at the end of your free report, guide, or webinar. Coupons, in particular, are so effective; we devote the next chapter to them…

Use Coupons

Coupons never grow old, though many businesses make the mistake of thinking this is an outdated technique, that it cheapens their brand, or that it would not work with their audience.

Did you know, statistically, millionaires are more like to use a coupon then someone on social welfare?

Coupons are used to give discounts, offer bonuses, provide free consultations, issue two for one offers, provide a free product or service upgrade, or give gifts. And they have been used for just about every product or industry you can imagine.

Before dismissing coupon codes, do a quick brainstorm on all the different ways you could use them in your own business.

They can increase the leads generated from your advertising or marketing and increase the conversions of those leads.

Here are a few tips for making coupon codes work well:

1) **Make them valuable.** A coupon code offering 50% off will get a much better response rate than one offering 5%. Of course, it needs to balance giving value with making financial sense, but if you are trying to stimulate new business, make the offer motivating.

2) **Have an expiration date.** A limit is needed for two reasons; firstly, you don't want people coming in five years from now trying to cash in an offer, and secondly, it gets people to take action. Time scarcity is a powerful motivator.

3) **Make it clear.** Having a coupon code is no good if people don't see it. Make your coupon stand out from your advert, email, or other marketing medium.

4) **Make it easy.** Some coupon codes are difficult to remember or difficult to use. Ensure a customer doesn't have to work hard to use it. Always test the process on a small group of subjects before rolling it out.

5) **Make it targeted.** Whatever you offer, make it relevant or targeted to the group of prospects you offer it to. All too often, companies offer something they think people will like but has nothing to do with their core product. Their offer might be appealing to some, but it will be appealing to far more if it is related.

Coupon codes can also be a great way to track individual advertising channel's effectiveness, or as a tool to track affiliate referrals. Simply create a unique code for each channel or affiliate.

In one software project I worked on, we used coupon codes to generate an extensive list of highly qualified prospects that generated over US$250,000 in under a week. To do this, we separated a single feature of the software, put a value of $37 on it, then created a coupon code that gave 100% off, but only if used within three days.

We then distributed the coupon codes through different social networks, to our lists, and via affiliates. The results were incredible.

A typical lead capture page (a landing page designed to capture the name and email of a qualified lead) converts at between 10–40%. Our system was converting at 84.2%—a previously unheard of result. The combination of targeting quality lead sources, offering a 100% discount, and having a three-day time limit meant that almost every person who visited the site took the offer.

We launched the core software to them a few days later, and the results speak for themselves.

There are many ways to use coupons, both online and off. One easy, low-cost suggestion is to print your offer on the back of a business card. You can then use a date stamp to add an expiration date on the card each time you give it out.

Depending on the offer, you can use these cards to stimulate new business, referrals, or repeat business.

Get creative. Coupons are an incredibly effective way of growing your business, is low cost, and take little time.

Search Engine Optimization (SEO)

Search engines can provide some of the lowest costing, highest converting leads of any marketing strategy.

When people search for specific phrases, they express an intent. That intent could be to research more about a specific topic, find a solution to a personal problem, or where to buy a particular product. The type of search term will determine the most effective approach to making a sale.

The most direct sale comes from someone looking for a product or service. These searchers use the internet to find the nearest, cheapest, or most trusted source. If you have what they are looking for, can meet their expectations, and can get their attention, then you have an excellent chance of making the sale.

This is the holy grail of marketing; to be in front of a highly qualified prospect right at the exact moment they want to buy—and without paying for expensive advertising.

Not that SEO is free. To be competitive, usually quite a bit of work is involved (depending on how much competition you have and how good they are). Besides, most searches are unlikely to be people wanting to buy that minute. They may not even know they want to buy anything at all.

General information searches are where a long play strategy is needed. Instead of getting product or service pages ranked, we try to rank content. This content will then provide the education we talked about before.

Content can provide reviews, product comparisons, answer FAQs, educate consumers about the differences between their options, or offer solutions to their problems. Instead of going straight for the sale (which would almost certainly be lost if we did), we build a relationship and become a trusted advisor.

This initial content will typically take the form of general web content, articles, blog posts, podcasts, PDFs, or video. We then aim to encourage the reader to revisit our site, subscribe to our email, or follow us on social media to continue the education process and deepen the relationship.

SEO is not a magic bullet, and you should never rely on it as your primary source of business. Google is just way too fickle for that. It is also not a technique that typically delivers results overnight. However, when done right, SEO can bring in an incredible ROI and generate some of the highest converting leads.

An effective SEO strategy can be broken down into three key areas: site structure, content, and backlinks.

Site Structure

This is the way your site is built and configured. It affects your site speed, how the search engines make sense of your website, and how information appears in the search results.

How much control you have over the structure will depend on which platform your website is built. Many, such as Wix, Weebly, and SquareSpace can be quite limited. Others, such as WordPress, are highly flexible. Most, however, at least give you some degree of control.

Some of the essential variables of site SEO include the structure and content of header tags (H1, H2, H3, etc.), meta description and title, images names and alt tags, URL structures, and internal links.

For most site owners, this is not something you need to worry about yourself. They should be done when the site is built. Just be aware that cheap sites are often cheap because they cut corners to save time (money) and don't bother to set these correctly. A lower-cost may land them the business and save you a few hundred dollars up front, but it will cost you far more in the long run.

In addition to these variables, site speed is also critical. The way the site is designed, the code is written and compressed, the images sized and compressed, and how data is cached all make a significant difference to how fast your site will load.

One of the most critical factors though, is the server used to host your site. If you are using a third-party service such as Wix, SquareSpace, or Shopify, you won't have any choice over the server. You get what you are given. If you are using

WordPress or Magento though, your choice of server is critical to your site's performance.

Unfortunately, most business owners do not fully appreciate the server's importance, and think that so long as their site works fine, then any will do. This lack of understanding leads to a choice based purely on price—which is a terrible mistake, as cheap hosting is cheap for a reason.

Low-cost hosting costs far more than it saves and is perhaps the most common form of false economy on the internet. I won't get into the technical here, but the bottom line is that your site's performance is compromised, which affects your SEO rankings, how much you pay for Google Ads, and how well your site converts.

Even an extra sale per month for most businesses would more than pay for a server upgrade, and yet most businesses are losing far more than that in an effort to keep costs low. Even when we explain this to business owners, most are still resistant to upgrade. This is nothing short of madness.

In one case we saw recently, sales virtually doubled by doing nothing more than changing server. Site speed is so important, we'll revisit it in the conversions section.

Content

All too often, we come across business owners who are afraid of having too much content. This belief is either due to personal preference or some VERY misguided advice. (Often from well-meaning friends, business mentors, or even web designers.)

Yet there is a common saying in SEO; 'content is king'. I can assure you, there is no such thing as too much content—so long as it is quality content: the more well-written, useful, relevant content, the better.

This advice is not based on personal opinion (unlike the poor advice mentioned above), but on years of testing and experience across countless businesses. And when you understand why, it makes total sense.

The usual logic given for having less information is that people are busy, lazy, or have short attention spans. And this is true. However, no one is forcing anyone to read everything. So long as your content is structured well, people who don't have the time or interest to read what you have written will simply skip it and buy anyway. There are, however, multiple reasons for more and longer pages of content.

Some of it has to do with conversions and some to do with SEO. We will look at the conversions side in the copywriting chapter in the next section, but for now, let's understand its importance for getting found in the search engines.

Search engines work to provide the best experience for their customer—the person searching, not business owners who all want their sites to rank. That means they need to show results that are relevant and useful.

Quality Traffic

To determine a good match, they use a large number of variables, many of which we cover in this chapter. Perhaps the most important variable of all though, is the content. Longer content has three crucial advantages over shorter content:

1) It contains more words and phrases that are relevant to your niche. These extra terms allow for more potential matches to what someone might search for. It also gives more statistical confidence to the search algorithms that your site is a good match.

2) The more content there is, the better chance you will be considered an authority site. If someone is researching a topic, they want depth, not just two lines. If someone is looking to buy a product, they often want to learn what they can about it, not just read the product name.

3) Google tracks the length of time people spend on your site, and how much they interact with it. If you have more content, then people will, on average, spend longer on your site. Time spent is seen as evidence that visitors find your site useful and engaging, and so you are rewarded by the search engine gods with a better position.

For many years, it was taught that you need three hundred and fifty to five hundred words for a blog post. Anything less than this was unlikely to rank. However, this is really at the low end. If your niche is competitive, then you will need to write much more.

A large SEO company recently measured how many words were on a page ranked number one for various search terms. The average was close to two thousand. And that was the average; some were well over three thousand words.

Of course, if people just came and were overwhelmed by the length of content, they would just bounce, and it would cause them to lose their position. The content needs to not only be long, but also laid out and written well. If it is just a long block of text, the font is too small, there are insufficient images, the text is too wide, or the information boring or irrelevant, most people will leave.

However, done well content is key to getting ranked well, and getting some of the lowest cost, highly qualified leads marketing can deliver.

Backlinks

A backlink is simply a link to your site from another website.

For a long time, backlinks were the foundation of search engine algorithms. The more, the better. While still important, over time, there has been a shift from quantity to quality. Indeed, some very low-quality backlinks can reduce your position, or even get you de-indexed altogether.

The golden rule is never to buy or swap backlinks. Doing so is considered a big no-no, and if you get caught, it could mean sudden death. Be very careful when hiring an agency to manage backlinking for you and be sure they don't build links from link farms or other underground sources.

The best quality links are from other authority sites, such as another highly ranked website in your niche or a government or recognised university website. These are, of course, not easy to get—but then, that is the point.

Luckily, most smaller businesses trying to get ranked locally won't need to go to these extremes. Getting listed on a variety of business directories and related trade websites or niche blogs will be sufficient.

The more contextually relevant the site is that links to yours, the better. One way to achieve this is to write high-quality articles or news pieces and submit them to online news sites or magazines. Just be sure to get a backlink in the author bio.

Having good quality content on your site can increase the chance that other websites will naturally link to yours as a useful resource. Good links like this can also provide organic traffic as people click on them.

The truth is, backlinking can be time-consuming (and tedious). The good news is that, precisely for these reasons, most of your competition won't bother doing it. By slowly adding backlinks over time, you can give yourself the edge and enjoy the extra business that a good SEO position provides.

Google My Business (GMB)

In many ways, Google My Business is just an extension to local SEO specific to Google search. GMB results are the local business listings we see at the top of Google's search page, often referred to as the three-pack.

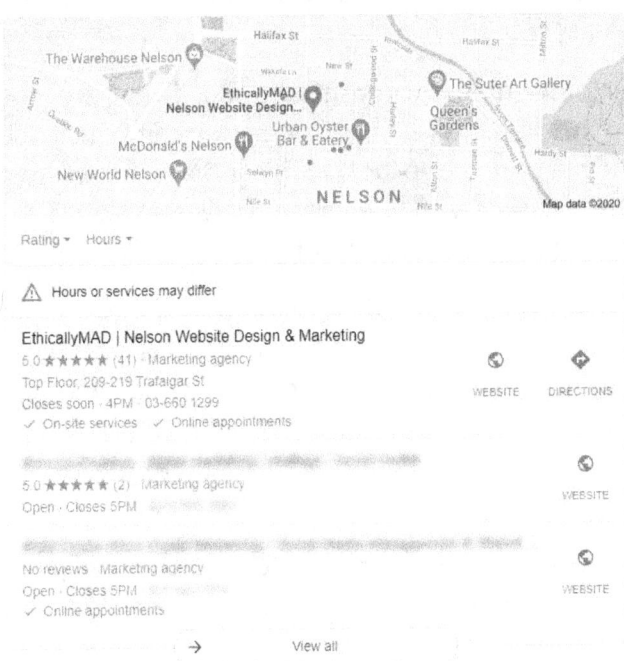

Getting inside this three-pack is perhaps the best possible use of a small, local businesses marketing budget. A GMB listing, setup well, will outperform natural SEO or Google Ad listings for searches focused on finding a local business. This is especially true for service-based businesses, such as lawyers, accountants, mechanics, plumbers, electricians, doctors, dentists, etc.

A lot of what is in the previous chapter on SEO applies here, but there are several unique factors to making a GMB listing work well. While we will cover the most important here, I will start by saying that you are far better off hiring a professional to do this for you (despite this being relatively easy).

There are only three top positions, and if you are not appearing in them, you can be sure your competition is getting the majority of the local business that is hot to trot. As most businesses try to do this themselves, it is not hard for a professional to do a better job and outrank them.

It is such an easy return on investment that we guarantee our services, and so should most other agencies offering to setup or manage GMB. (One business we worked with got an additional twelve thousand dollars of business in the first week alone.) That said, here are a few of the essentials to be sure to get done.

Complete profile: There are quite a few fields to complete when setting up your Google My Business listing. Be sure to complete them all. The more information you provide, the more Google sees you are serious about your business, and the better your listing will look.

Of particular importance is the category and sub-category under which you choose to list your business. The category choice significantly impacts whether your listing shows in the most relevant searches (or not).

Images: Regardless of your business, images can help your listing. Avoid stock images and keep photos relevant to your business. Product shots, shots of your office or store, team photos etc. are all good to post.

Your reviews: As you will notice in our GMB listing screenshot, we have five stars based on significantly more reviews than the competition. This is not by accident. We actively request all our customers to leave a review (and aim always to deliver a five-star service).

Getting the most or best reviews won't guarantee you the top spot, but it certainly helps get you more clicks and increases trust.

It is also beneficial to reply to all the reviews, good and bad. It shows both Google and prospective clients you care and are actively engaged. Should you have a disgruntled customer or a fake review (they happen), how you handle the response becomes more important than the review itself.

Keywords: Using the right words in your title and description will help Google identify who to show your listing to, and help people see how relevant it is to what they are searching for.

Choosing the right keywords may sound obvious, but it never ceases to amaze us how often we see poorly written listings.

List your products or services: GMB gives you the ability to list what you offer. Your listing can provide valuable information for someone exploring your profile, as well as give Google additional information to help define how to rank you.

Regular updates: Google knows that businesses change or die over time. By updating your listing regularly, you demonstrate you are both still in business, and the information in your listing is valid.

It is not only images that should be updated often. Changing your opening times for public holidays, adding or editing your products or services, creating events, adding articles or blog posts, or merely replying to reviews or messages all show you are still active.

Aim to make at least one or two updates each month, though ideally weekly. If, like most business owners, you are too busy or hate this type of activity, then make sure someone else does it, or hire a professional. I can't emphasise enough just how important this is.

If you are unsure if your profile is setup well, get in touch, and we will be happy to check for you at no cost. Message us at
www.ethciallymad.co.nz/contact.

Onsite Conversions

Onsite Conversions

Messaging

The most common mistake we see on websites is poor messaging. It is such a simple thing to fix and makes an incredible difference, yet few businesses take the time to get it right. The truth is—many companies are not even sure what their message is.

Your message is key to everything. I define marketing as 'the communication of your message'. When you lack a clear, strong, and emotionally engaging message, your marketing will suffer.

If all you have to say is "buy from us, we are the best or cheapest" or use other unquantifiable terms such as 'quality', 'leading' or 'value', your message will be lost in the sea of other boring, meaningless, and clichéd terms. Bottom line is—few people who hear it will care.

Worse, well over half of all messages we see are so unclear, prospects are not even sure what the business is offering. If you don't believe me, test it for yourself. Have someone who knows nothing about your business visit your website, give them four to five seconds to look at it, then ask them what exactly you offer, and what your point of difference is.

Think this is unfair? A few seconds is about how long people spend to decide if your site has what they are looking for, if they trust you, and whether you look like you are worth the time to compare against the competition.

Ethical Marketing

You need to craft a message that gets people to care. When they care, they are more likely to learn more, buy from you, and tell others about you. (Getting people to care also increases the number of people who want to work for you or do business with you.)

The power of getting people to care about your message should not be underestimated. This is *one* reason we love to work with social enterprises—they have a clear purpose beyond just profit. Having a purpose makes crafting a message people care about and respond to so much easier.

Your message should be as concise as possible, ideally just a headline, or a headline and sub-headline.

Make sure it is clear what you do and what your core point of difference is. This difference should offer some benefit to the reader, such as lower cost, time-saving, extra service, certainty in the form of a guarantee, or a feel-good factor due to your social or environmental impact.

If you are a specialist in a particular area, then make that clear. In many fields, people often trust a specialist more and are willing to pay a premium to work with one. Yet all too often, they need to dig deep to find this information. If it is relevant, give it to them upfront.

Onsite Conversions

Copywriting

Copy is the words on your website. Copywriting has been described as 'salesmanship in print', and it is fundamental to converting leads to sales. Yet over 95% of site owners do not want to invest in getting it done professionally.

The typical attitude is that copywriting is a luxury expense where savings can be made. The underlying belief being that words are words, and almost anyone can write, and if someone wants to buy, they will.

This attitude is exceptionally foolish. Copywriting may well be one of the most essential components to your website, your marketing, and your potential business success. Unfortunately, good copywriting is rare, and seldom included as part of a website quote.

So why is good copy so expensive, yet one of the best investments you will ever make?

Any good car yard knows the importance of an outstanding salesman. On any given day, they will have the same stock and the same average quality of leads. The yard can have several guys wearing identical suits, yet one will outperform the others by a considerable margin.

How so? If the logic that customers will buy if they find what they are looking for or that external appearances or branding are all that is important, then the results should be the same. But they're not.

High performing sales professionals in every industry know the importance of training. Training that teaches them what to say, what not to say, how to say it, when to say it, how to manage objections, and how to close.

Yet if a website fails to do the same, the prospect is likely never to call or visit your business. And if you are making sales online, then you will lose the customer to your competition.

Just look at your own behaviour. No doubt you have searched for products and services online. You visit a website, only to choose one of its competitors, despite it having what you needed.

What influenced your decision?

There will have been several factors, but one of the biggest is likely to be what you read (or did not read). The same is true for your site visitors. They have landed on your site for a reason, so it's your site's job to give them the information they are looking for and, ultimately, get them to take a desired action (buy, book, call, visit, donate, etc.).

Too many sites use stuffy corporate language in an effort to look more 'professional'. Others are just written so poorly that it makes them look unprofessional. Neither will work as well as a friendly tone that uses the language of the intended audience, and which has been professionally edited.

It is crucial not just to provide the information people want but also to engage them emotionally, build trust, and develop a personal connection. Very much the same as a good salesperson does.

Like a salesperson, to do this well requires training and practice.

I have written copy for sales pages that have generated millions in sales. For the pages that have converted the best and made the most, I spend weeks writing and crafting them. Not hours, or even days, but weeks.

Why take so long?

To write copy well requires researching and understanding the product, the competition, and the customer. It then takes time to write, and far more time again to edit and re-edit. Copy may need to be edited nine or ten times before it is excellent, sometimes more. This all takes time.

However, this is time very well spent. Just like a lousy salesperson, lousy copy will lose you sales. If you have paid to get a visitor to your website, this is lost revenue and money down the drain. Conversely, the better the copy, the more sales you make, the better your return on ad spend.

However, unlike a salesperson, you only need to pay for good copywriting once. After this, it continues to work for you twenty-four-seven. Now, that is what I call a good investment.

Therefore, I find it crazy that so many business owners will not hesitate to hire sales staff, but they won't invest in perfecting the words that many more people see and that gives a much better return.

One of the recurring themes in this book, is the idea that you should never measure the cost of something based only on the dollar amount. Always look at the return. Small business that fail to understand this, stay small.

Even if good copywriting could be done in three hours rather than three weeks, it would still be just as profitable an investment. It really does not matter how long it takes; it only matters that the money you make is far more than the money you spend. Good copy will do just that.

Non-profits may be thinking this does not apply to them. Social causes may not always measure profit as a return on investment, but they should always measure some Social Impact Metric to see what return they get for their spend.

Assuming that, as a non-profit, you are looking to increase donations, recruit volunteers, or educate people, then good copy can be just as important (and, from a social perspective, more important).

As with the rest of a well-designed website, good copy is a tool to get better leverage on your other marketing and advertising spend.

While I always suggest hiring a good copywriter, it is still essential to have a solid foundation in good copy. If not, you may not recognise good copy from bad. It is also instrumental in all your communication, from sales email

Onsite Conversions

and social media posts to internal company communication and job listings.

To give yourself a solid grounding in this fine art, I highly recommend *'Ca$hvertising'* by Drew Eric Whitman. This book is by far one of the most comprehensive and easy to read on the subject.

Offer an Insane Guarantee

A crucial component to making a sale is removing risk.

When you have what someone wants at a price they can afford, the biggest obstacle to making the sale is almost always fear. Most people fear making the wrong decision, especially when it comes to spending money. (Which is why so many people procrastinate or avoid paying for marketing!)

Building trust helps reduce this fear, but a solid guarantee can smash it. It also can help smash your competition...

A perfect example of this is the guarantee that took Dominos Pizza from an almost unheard-of brand to the second-largest pizza chain in America. At a time when home delivery pizza was known for being slow and cold, they offered a 'hot in under thirty minutes or it's free' promise.

If you wanted a hot pizza in a reasonable timeframe, this was a guarantee that could not be ignored. And you had little to lose, because if Dominos failed in their promise, you got it for free.

It amazes me how many businesses have the opportunity to dominate their competition simply by out guaranteeing them—yet are too afraid. I hear all sorts of excuses as to why this strategy won't work; "you don't understand, people will take advantage of us", "my business advisor has told us it will cheapen our brand", "our customers would not respond to that", or "it would be too difficult to manage"—all fear.

None of these objections are from experience or testing. They are just opinions. Personally, I am interested in the opinions of the people who have tried and tested what they are advising on. And in this case, the evidence is clear. Strong guarantees work.

Yes, there will likely be some refunds, and some sales may end up costing money. But the cost of honouring a strong guarantee does not come close to the extra profit it generates.

Many years back, I used to be a therapist. It was during this time that I first came across the concept of a strong guarantee, and decided to give it a try. I offered a no result, no pay guarantee. As soon as I did, bookings increased; but not once did anyone take me up on it. I have used them ever since.

My advice... Go crazy. Come up with something outstanding and test it for yourself. You have little to lose and potentially a whole lot of business to gain. You can always remove the guarantee if you don't like the result.

Use Testimonials and Reviews

Another way to increase trust and minimize people's fear of making the wrong buying decision is to use testimonials and reviews.

Apart from not having any testimonials, the most common mistake that most businesses make is to hide them on a dedicated page called testimonials, then list them out as a pile of unappealing text. This is a real waste of marketing gold.

Don't rely on people clicking a link to read through testimonials—few do. Instead, spread them throughout your site, and make sure they are attractive and easy to read. If you can, include the name of the person giving the testimonial, the city they are from, and their photo (whenever possible).

The more testimonials you include, and the more places you put them, the greater the odds they will get seen. Even a short, punchy testimonial under the complete checkout button can decrease the abandon cart rate (number of people who do not complete a purchase).

If you want to increase viewer's trust in your testimonials, then pull them from Google, Facebook, or TripAdvisor. By connecting your site to display the testimonials from any of these sources, visitors are more confident they are genuine.

Onsite Conversions

A review from a recognised authority or celebrity also adds a lot of credibility, and therefore trust, to your business. While celebrities will often charge for their endorsement, this is not always the case—especially when they believe in what you do.

If you have a high-quality product, a review from a recognized authority in your industry is another excellent form of endorsement, and often easier to get than you may expect. Simply send a sample to them, and ask for their feedback. Be sure to ask if they are happy for you to use that feedback publicly. Many industry experts are more than willing, as it helps increase their profile too.

Regardless of whether you are asking for a customer testimonial, a celebrity endorsement, or a professional review, being clear on your social and environmental impact can help get others on board without financial or other personal incentives.

Usability

Far too many websites only fail because they are hard to use. Usability issues include being difficult to read, challenging to navigate, having complex forms or checkout processes, or lacking the information people are looking for in places they expect to find it.

Business owners tend to expect their web designer to have taken care of these basic requirements, yet few do. Designers are rarely trained in usability (and programmers certainly aren't); others simply do not consider function as necessary as design.

If you want conversions, consider both function and design need. Never compromise Important functionality in the pursuit of making the site look good. People visit your site because they want information or buy something from you—they are not there to admire your work of art (unless you sell art, but even then, they need to navigate effortlessly to buy it).

Common usability mistakes include text that is too small or wide, centring large blocks of text, low contrast (such as putting grey text on a grey background), having long paragraphs, or having strong background images that make text unclear. Text is there for a reason—for people to read it. Make it as easy as possible or most just won't bother.

Readability is made worse when there are many font types, sizes, and colours. Try to limit your site to no more than two or three font styles, two or three font sizes, and two or three colours.

Be sure to use the same font styles consistently throughout the site too. For example, all headlines should follow the same format, use the same for sub-headlines, body copy, and links, etc.

Poor navigation is another common problem. Always put menus in a location and format with which people are familiar. Fancy menus may look cool or feel clever, but they almost always result in frustration for the user, and lost business for the owner.

We try to limit the number of options in the main menu to no more than four or five links. More links than this can feel overwhelming, and people rarely see the different options. Instead, they scan the beginning and end links while missing the middle ones.

Testing for usability issues takes time, but getting valuable feedback is relatively easy to do. You just need four or five people who know nothing about your business or your website, a computer connected to your website, and thirty minutes or so with each of your test subjects.

Take one at a time, and explain you want them to look at a website and answer the following questions:

1) What products or services does the site offer?

2) What is the site's key selling point or point of difference?

3) Can you clearly see how to navigate or take a desired action (such as buy or book)?

4) Does the site look trustworthy?

Next, have them look at your homepage for just five seconds. This short time is all it should take to answer the above questions—if it has been designed well. Most people visiting your site will make most of these judgements in less time than this, and their patience is limited.

After this initial short quiz, have your test subjects complete a series of quick tasks. These should include finding specific information that people may need to make a buying decision, fill in a contact form, find your phone number, or make a booking or purchase.

As they do, watch their actions without giving any assistance. This way, you can see where they become lost, get confused, or get stuck. Take note of any observations. These are all areas to improve. You may even want to record their actions using a camera to watch back or show to other members of your team.

Once they have finished, have them answer a few more simple questions. These may include:

- What did you find most challenging or confusing when using the site?

- What would you like to see improved?

- What would make you consider purchasing from this business?

- What would stop you from purchasing from this business?

- Was there anything that made this business stand out from the competition? If so, what?

- Was there any information or functionality that you didn't see that you would like added?

- Do you have any other feedback or suggestions?

Try not to overwhelm your guinea pigs with questions but be sure to ask enough to get sufficient information to improve your site's performance.

This process does not take long, but it can provide valuable insight that could save you a fortune in lost sales. If you don't have time to conduct this research yourself, then contract someone else to do it for you—either way, don't miss this valuable step, as it will return far more than it costs.

Design

Aesthetics are important, though not as important as many people (especially designers and site owners) think. There have been many tests done that show an ugly site outperforming a sexy version. This is not because ugly is better, but because many design decisions compromise readability and usability, which reduce conversions.

Design choices should be based less on preference and more on what will increase sales. A professional-looking design will increase trust, but this is only one small part of what it takes to convert a visitor.

Some common design mistakes include:

Headline and button colours. All too often, designers try to make the colours of headlines and buttons blend in. Testing has shown that conversions increase when these elements pop from the page.

These results do not mean you should just use any bright colour. A good designer will know how to select a colour that complements the colours and tones used throughout your site while still grabbing attention.

Using sliders. Sliders are those large images that rotate, typically used at the top of the page. Many web designers love them—but you should hate them! Simply put, they kill conversions.

Onsite Conversions

Don't believe me? Google 'sliders kill conversions', and you will see test after test from leading experts that prove sliders are bad for business. I could write an entire chapter on why, but I won't. Just don't use them, and if your web designer tries, stop them!

Using hamburger menus on desktop sites. Hamburger menus, typically used on mobile sites, confuse many visitors using non-mobile devices. This advice may change in the future due to an increasing number of sites using them, but it is not good practice for now.

Designers love them because they clean up messy looking menus, but they are a lazy option. Using a classic menu structure makes your site easy to navigate. Just be sure to not have too many options in the primary navigation as visitors can become overwhelmed.

Complex design. Sites that have a lot visually going on can be a nightmare to use. Many can look aesthetically appealing (when done well), but the eye does not know where to look.

Use plenty of blank space around elements (such as menus, headlines, images, videos, button, text blocks, etc.) to help the viewer separate the various parts of the page. The extra padding makes it much easier for them to find what they are looking for, and direct them to what you want them to see.

Live Chat

Live chat is that little icon in the bottom left corner that pops up when you visit a site and allows you to chat directly with customer support. It is an easy way to increase sales and can be free to implement.

Just having it on your site has been shown to increase both form submissions and sales—even when people have not engaged with the live chat function. It is assumed this is because just having it increases people's confidence that they can speak to someone should there ever be a problem.

Even if your business is small and has no full-time support staff, no need to worry. Most chat systems offer a mobile app so you can get messages directly to your phone. You can also set up automated replies to answer common questions or capture visitor details to follow up with when you get time.

It is surprising the number of additional enquiries you get by having a live chat system. It just encourages more people to contact you, and with the right message in the chat popup, you can engage visitors who may have otherwise left without contacting you.

There are many different systems out there, but one we use on many projects is *www.tawk.to*. They have a robust free option, a great business philosophy, and their system works well too.

Onsite Conversions

If you are using HubSpot, ActiveCampaign, or another similar system that offers an integrated chat system, it is usually a good idea to use their inbuilt solution.

Dedicated Landing Pages

Many businesses send all their leads to their site's homepage, but this can be a big mistake.

By building unique pages for different visitor sources, you can target the content to their needs, and in doing so, dramatically increase conversions. It is a strategy that takes time but is well worth it.

Let's say you are a digital marketer with a range of services, and you are using Google Ads to drive traffic to your website. If someone searches for 'web design', then you want to send that person directly to your page on web design. If they are searching for 'marketing consultant', you want to send them directly to the page selling your consultancy services.

While it is, of course, possible for someone to find the relevant page from a well-designed homepage, every unnecessary step removed will help improve results. More than just simplifying things for the user, a landing page also allows us to hyper-target our message.

For example, if you have a weight loss programme and someone searches 'post-pregnancy weight loss programme', you can direct them to a page that talks specifically to that demographic. The solution may be the same, but the sales message is not—at least not if you want maximum conversions.

Onsite Conversions

The benefit of a landing page holds true for offline advertising too. If you placed your weight loss ad in a women's magazine, you would want to send readers to a different page than the ad placed in a men's magazine. Just as a good car salesperson will customize his or her sales pitch to the buyer in front of them, you should do your best to craft sales copy to match your prospect. A landing page is one way to do just this.

There is another advantage to using a landing page over your home page… you can create specific calls to action. A home page usually needs to sell your overall message and act as a point of navigation to help visitors find the information or product they are looking for. If you already know what they want, you can ensure that the landing page has a call to action to meet their needs.

If you know someone is ready to buy, your landing page will likely be a sales page, focused on selling your visitor a specific product or service (e.g., digital marketing consultancy). If they are searching for information, it could be a chance to capture their name and email address in exchange for a free report or short e-course, so you follow up with them and sell them on your paid products later.

Landing pages are so effective, that in many cases, they not only increase the return from a campaign, but make an advertising channel financially viable. Many businesses throw money away on advertising because the ads cost more than they earn. Sending leads to such a targeted page can increase conversions to the point where the same ads return a healthy profit.

Onsite Conversions

Site Speed

As mentioned before, the time it takes your website to load can significantly impact your bottom line. Most people do not appreciate just how significant an impact.

Research conducted by Akamai found that a two-second increase in loading time more than doubled the people who left the site without taking any action. Another study by skilled.co found sites taking 2.4 seconds to load converted at an average of 1.9%, while those taking 4.2 seconds converted at less than 1%. An increase of just 1.8 seconds could be losing you half of all your sales!

You should remember that a 50% drop in sales is much more than a 50% drop in profit. Your advertising and operating costs remain the same, so for many businesses, this will mean the difference between substantial growth and going under.

It gets worse though...

Google understands visitors hate slow sites, especially on mobile. Their job is to make sure people using their search service find the sites they want—no matter if that is by clicking on an organic listing or a paid ad, which is why they penalise slow sites.

This penalisation affects businesses in two crucial ways. Firstly, it will make it much harder for a website to rank well in Google's natural search results. A lower position can mean less highly qualified visitors to your site, and so—even fewer sales. This is especially true for mobile searches.

Secondly, if you are using Google Ads, you will have to pay more for each click than if your site is running faster. This increased cost will make it harder to compete, and at the very least will increase your customer acquisition cost (therefore further reducing your profit on any sales).

As you can see, this creates a compound effect—fewer visits to your site and fewer sales from those who do make it. Conversely, if you can increase your site speed, you can expect more visitors, lower Google Ad spend, and an increase in conversions.

It is important to remember that conversions don't just affect online sales. Conversions include phone calls, online enquiries or bookings, and visits to your store or office, as well as having people read your information or message.

In short, speed matters. Check yours now by visiting *https://developers.google.com/speed/pagespeed/insights*.

Onsite Conversions

Conversion Rate Optimisation

Too many sites are built or rebuilt, then left. Business owners (or marketers who should know better) believe that a website is a one-off expense that can be paid for then left to do its thing.

And, for sites that get little traffic, this may as well be true. But if you are getting a few thousand hits per month, you should seriously consider CRO (conversion rate optimisation). If you are getting tens of thousands of visitors, then CRO is a must.

CRO is a systematic approach to increasing conversion rates through scientific experimentation of the many ideas contained in this book, along with a host of others. Just about every successful business with a strong online presence uses it. This is no coincidence.

Regardless of how well designed a website is or how well it is written, the chances are it is not performing as well as it could. When you have ten thousand visits in a month, a small percentage improvement can make a big difference. Bear with me as we run some basic numbers—it may just be the most important thing you learn about having a business or project website.

If you can increase your conversion rate from 1% to 1.1%, it may not sound significant, but let's take a closer look...

Ethical Marketing

With ten thousand visitors, a 1% conversion rate will equate to 100 sales, while a 1.1% conversion rate will result in 110 sales. To keep the numbers simple, let's say an average sale brings in $150. Of that $150, $50 is raw cost, $40 is marketing costs, $10 covers overheads, and $50 is net profit. That means 100 sales make you $5,000.

However, 110 sales look a little different. Your overheads and marketing cost were the same, so they are covered. Therefore, the cost of delivering the extra ten sales is just the raw cost. That means you are making $100 profit on each of those new sales. So, these extra sales result in an additional $1,000 in net profit. That is a twenty percent increase in profit for adding 0.1% to the conversion rate.

Now, let's see what happens when we double our ad spend and get twice the number of visits to our site. In the first scenario, we will go from $5,000 monthly net profit to $10,000. But with the increased conversion rates, we are now making $12,000 each month. An extra $2,000 per month over the year means an additional $24,000 annual net profit.

The best part—the cost of the optimisation will keep providing a positive return year after year. Over ten years, this would bring the business an additional $240,000. Not bad.

However, these numbers are quite conservative. Let's rerun those numbers for a larger business that is getting 100,000 visits with a sale price of $450. We will keep the same rough margins, i.e., $150 for raw cost, $150 for

Onsite Conversions

marketing and overheads, and $150 for profit. This means that at a 1% conversion rate, they are making 1,000 sales with $450,000 in revenue and $150,000 in profit.

With a bit of extra testing and improvement, it is relatively easy to take the conversion rate from 1% to 1.2%. That means an additional 200 sales, all at $300 profit rather than $150 (remember the overheads and marketing costs were covered in the first 1,000 sales). The increased conversions mean an extra $60,000 in profit—a 40% increase in profits.

That's $720,000 more per year, or a cool $7.2 million over ten years—all with only 0.2% difference in conversions.

Now, imagine if that additional revenue was re-invested into company growth. It would have a compound effect that would mean, over time, the real numbers over time would be much higher again.

What's exciting is that increasing conversions by 0.2% is surprisingly easy for most sites. Many have taken conversion rates from less than 1% to over 3% or even 4%—that's 300 or 400% growth in revenues, and even more in profits. Using this approach, you can see why some companies can achieve massive growth in a relatively short time.

With most offline business's transactions starting with an online search, online conversions rates affect just about every business. The bad news is that if your competition is doing CRO and you are not, they will dominate you. It is only a matter of time.

The good news is that many businesses still don't understand the importance of CRO, and so are not doing it. Not doing CRO is crazy when there is so much at stake.

CRO follows a relatively simple process. Instead of rebuilding a new site from the ground up, changes are made incrementally. You can improve any page by creating a second variation of it, with a variation of the element you wish to test.

For example, if you want to improve your homepage headline, you can use a split testing program (such as Google Optimise) to try different headlines and see which converts the best. If you test just two versions, it is known as an A/B split test. If you test more than two, it is known as multivariate testing. Unless you have high amounts of traffic to your site, A/B is generally best as it will give you a result much faster.

Of course, it is not just headlines—you can test colours, layouts, button text, page copy, images, videos, etc. I won't detail here how to do CRO, as this needs a book unto itself. Due to the skill range and tools required to do CRO, it is generally more cost-effective to outsource or subcontract the work. However, as you can see, the returns are well worth the investment.

Onsite Conversions

Better Decisions Through Metrics

While not technically a strategy for directly increasing revenue or other forms of impact, measuring metrics allows you to see progress, track what works and what doesn't, and often gives unexpected insights. Online, it is possible to track extremely detailed data. Data that, in the past, companies paid hundreds of thousands to collect is now available for free.

Using tools such as Google Analytics, we can see which source visitors came from, what they were searching for before arriving on our site, which city they are in, their age and gender, which types of traffic convert, how long people spend on each page, which pages visitors exit from, and so much more.

This data can prove invaluable in decision making. Take one client of ours who was about to increase spending on his Facebook marketing. He knew Facebook was sending him a lot of visitors, so he figured that devoting more money to it would increase traffic to his site. And he was probably right. The only problem, none of the Facebook visitors were buying.

On the other hand, Pinterest was bringing in very little traffic, but the traffic it did bring was generating sales. This valuable information saved him from throwing money away and instead enabled him to invest in a high converting traffic source.

Heat mapping is another valuable source of data. Heat maps visually show you how people are interacting with your pages. You can see how many people scroll, their mouse movements, and where on the screen they are clicking. With this information, it is possible to see where to focus and make quick wins.

To help see the big picture with your data, we also recommend a tool such as Octoboard. This tool enables you to bring together and display data from multiple sources, such as Google Analytics, Google Ads, Facebook, MailChimp, Xero, and many others. You can also mashup data from the different sources for deeper insights.

A word of warning with Google Analytics... it is straightforward to add Google's tracking code. However, to get quality data requires a bit more work. You need to add filters to remove unwanted data, such as bot traffic. You also need to set up Google Tag Manager to track button clicks, form submissions, the number of video plays etc. Finally connect your account to Google Search Console for better SEO insights, and set up goal tracking.

Learning how to do it well takes time, so this is one of those tasks you will want to get done professionally—not that I am biased ;-)

In our experience, less than ten percent of businesses have their analytics set up well. Most web designers or developers will add the code, but few know how to configure everything well. Make sure you use an analytics specialist for this.

Onsite Conversions

(If you need some help, check out our analytics set up packages at,
www.EthicallyMAD.co.nz/analytics.)

Follow Up

Follow Up

Stalking Professionally

Every sales professional knows that only a small percentage of sales are made on the first point of contact. It is no different for websites. The vast majority of visitors to your site will leave, never to return—even those who want what you have.

If you assume prospects will come back when they are ready to buy, you'll be wrong far more often than you're right. Just look at your own behaviour when visiting other websites. It's nothing personal, just that you are not in the right time or place to make a buying decision, may not have enough information or trust, or get distracted and forget to complete the transaction.

There are many reasons why people don't buy on the first visit (and far fewer why they will). While we can design the site to reduce resistance as much as possible, most visitors still don't buy on the first visit, and won't return—unless we follow up with them.

Thankfully, due to the power of digital marketing, there are numerous options available to us. Each one is powerful on its own, but you dramatically increase your chances of making a sale when used in combination. Let's take a look at each…

Email

Email is the oldest of all the online follow-up methods, and (if done right) still the most effective. However, you need to capture the visitor's email address before sending any messages to them. Collecting email is a challenge in itself, but it is usually much easier than making a direct sale, and well worth the effort.

To make email effective, you must capture the details of as many visitors as possible. You must also have an effective follow-up sequence. With no one to send to, the best email campaign in the world won't help you. And with no email campaign, the largest email list in the world won't help either.

The most common mistake I see when building a list is merely offering a newsletter or 'updates'. This is not 1998. Few people want more newsletters in their inbox. This ineffectiveness is made worse when the only place you can sign up for the newsletter is a tiny form hidden in the site's footer—where less than fifty percent of people even look.

Make sure you offer something of value; at least a coupon code, a free report, an e-course, a webinar, a free consultation, or a free trial—something that will provide relevant value to a qualified prospect.

A newsletter in the footer will typically get less than one percent of all visitors to opt-in. A well-designed landing page or pop up can get opt-in rates from ten to forty percent. (On one project, we designed an advanced strategy that achieved an opt-in rate of over 82%.) The better your opt-in rate, the more visitors you have to follow up and convert to customers.

When designing an email campaign, you should harness the power of the BEAST. That is the five types of email, Broadcast, Event, Autoresponder, Support, and Transactional. Each has its potential to increase sales, so let's dive into more detail…

Broadcast

Broadcast messages are one-off emails, such as product launch announcements, newsletters, product updates, and one-off promotions. They are sent once, and if someone is not on your list when you send the email, they will never receive it.

There are endless ways to use this type of email, and they form a vital part of any ongoing digital marketing campaign. Their downside, however, is that they also require constant work. You need to create a new email each time you want a result.

On the plus side, I have used them many times to generate quick cash (which has saved needing to take a loan or seek investment when growing a business), maintain a relationship with customers by keeping them up-to-date, and conduct valuable research by sending out questionnaires.

Once you have a good, quality list, especially previous customers, the return you get on sending out a well-written email is hard to beat. (One email I wrote took no more than five minutes and made over $15,000 within twenty minutes of sending.)

Event

Event-triggered emails are sent when someone interacts with your site or app in a specific way. Perhaps the most well-known and well-used event email is the abandon shopping cart message. These are sent when a prospect fills out a checkout form but does not complete the purchase.

The email is sent anywhere from an hour to a day later, reminding them to complete the transaction or asking if there was any difficulty making the purchase. Cart abandonment rates vary dramatically from fifteen to eighty percent (up to eighty-five percent on mobile). Of those, a well-written email can recover approximately ten to twenty percent of those otherwise lost sales.

The effectiveness of abandoned cart email depends on the traffic source, sales process, transaction value, email copy, device someone is using, along with a myriad of other variables (such as location and time of day etc.).

Regardless of your exact numbers though, it's crazy not to have an abandoned cart recovery email. It takes a few minutes to set up and will continue to work for you for years to come. Over time, those recovered sales provide an excellent return for the tiny cost of setting up and running the email.

There are many other forms of event-based email, many of them quite advanced, but for any e-commerce store, this should be the first one to add.

Autoresponders

The autoresponder is an email technology that has been the backbone of digital marketing for over twenty years. (Despite being underutilised by virtually every business we have consulted for.)

Having a well-built autoresponder has been likened to having a sales team working almost for free 24/7 and described as a license to print money.

So, what makes autoresponders just so powerful?

Part of the answer lies within the name, *auto*-responder. Put simply, an autoresponder automates the sending of email sequences. Its real power though, is combining this automated sending with targeting and a well-designed strategy.

Unlike a broadcast email, email in an autoresponder sequence are sent again and again over time. When someone new is added to a list, they will receive the first email, then after a set period, they receive the second, and so on.

Once set up, autoresponders do all the hard work for you year in, year out, and at a fraction of an employee's cost. To improve results from your email sequences, split test your messages. Use the test results to keep tweaking or adding new messages. However, even if you just set and forget, you should still see great returns.

You can use an autoresponder for various purposes, including educating, building trust, asking for reviews or referrals, running automated offers, upselling other products, recommending affiliate offers, delivering e-courses, etc.

Their flexibility makes them perfectly suited to following up with new leads and handholding them through the process to become a new customer. It also makes them perfect for building that relationship further and encourage them to become a repeat buyer.

Many businesses fail with autoresponders for one or more of the following reasons:

1) Too much selling, not enough value. It is vital to build a relationship with valuable content or resources. If all you do is sell, people will soon unsubscribe.

2) Not having enough email. While you don't want to be sending an email every day, most businesses don't send anywhere near enough. Quality and quantity, not one or the other. Within reason, the more emails you send (over time), the more you will make.

Follow Up

3) Sending poorly written emails. I am not talking about grammar that would make your English teacher proud. I am talking about well thought out, with excellent copywriting. The better your copy, the better the response will be. (Be warned… people with excellent English skills often write terrible copy.)

4) Poor targeting. To get the best results, filter your list to ensure you send emails relevant to the recipient. Most autoresponders offer some impressive list filtering options, and while requiring a bit of extra setup, the additional time is well spent. For example, filter anyone who already has purchased a product you are promoting.

Support

If someone contacts your support desk, there is a high probability they want your reply. The fact that they initiated the contact means support email enjoy very high open and read rates. These email may include customer help requests, sales enquiries, feedback, or complaints.

No matter what the reason for a support email, treat each as a marketing opportunity. At the very least, you can have a marketing message in your email footer promoting your latest offer or requesting testimonials or a referral. If someone is having problems or making a complaint, give them a coupon code or a gift as a way of apology.

Remember, marketing is not just about trying to make a quick sale but about building a relationship. How you manage people when they are unhappy can lead to either more unhappiness or a raving fan.

Transactional

Typically, these are emails sent when someone makes a purchase and can include purchase confirmation, receipts, invoices, shipping updates, or login details. Again, these have very high open rates, and are missed opportunities by most businesses.

In the offline world, supermarkets have long taken advantage of a receipt's marketing potential. At the bottom, you will often find a discount coupon for a future purchase or an offer for cheap fuel—you can be sure both are there to make the supermarket more money. There is no reason not to do the same in an email or invoice attachment.

Give yourself an email audit. Take a look through the email you are currently using in your business and see what you can add or improve. Get creative. Try finding how many ways you can use email to enhance your business in a variety of ways.

For business driven by purpose, email offers an incredible, low-cost opportunity to promote your message, or request post shares, likes, signatures on a petition, or other forms of direct action from your list.

The better you use email, the more profitable your business will be, and the greater impact it will have.

Follow Up

Retargeting

This proven strategy has been around for years, yet it is still not used by most businesses. Of those that do use retargeting (sometimes called remarketing), few do it well. To not use retargeting is a missed opportunity, as it is not unusual for a business to more than double its investment when it does.

Retargeting requires a lead to visit your website before they start seeing your ads. No doubt you have had this experience before—you visit a website only to be followed around for days or weeks by their ads.

It is important to remember that retargeting won't generate new leads. Instead, it follows up and helps convert more of the leads that would have otherwise visited your site never to come back.

One of the reasons retargeting has an excellent ROI is because if someone has already been to your site and were not interested in what you had to offer, they are unlikely to click on your ad again. If you are only paying for the click, it means you are only paying for hyper-qualified leads.

With retargeting ads, you can remind visitors you exist, entice them back with a special offer, increase trust by showing testimonials, or make an offer to bring them to an opt-in page (and so have them enter your email marketing machine).

Several platforms offer retargeting, including Google Ads, Facebook and Twitter. Each requires you to put tracking code on your site, so they know who to show your ads.

An alternative is to use a service such as Adroll. With Adroll, you only need one account, one lot of setup, and one tracking code. It then displays your ads across over two hundred platforms, including Google, Facebook, Microsoft and Yahoo.

As with email marketing, you will want to create filters to remove anyone who clicks on your ad, or maybe has visited a particular page (e.g. order complete), so that you are not wasting your ads on people who have bought or won't buy.

Also, consider how long you want to keep showing ads to a lead. The length of time will generally depend on the typical buying cycle for your product or service. If you are an emergency plumber, that cycle is going to be very short. If you are selling cars, it is likely to be much longer. You want to ensure your ads remain visible for as long as it takes people to make a buying decision.

Follow Up

Social Media

Another simple way to follow up with leads is via social media. Before we get started on this topic, it is essential to distinguish between social media and advertising on social media, as the two are often confused.

Facebook Ads, Twitter Ads, LinkedIn Ads etc., are all advertising. This is a legitimate marketing strategy, but it is not social media. (In the same way, putting an ad in a newspaper does not make you a journalist.)

Unfortunately, social media is not quite as effective as many social media gurus or the marketing hype would have you believe—and it is nowhere near as effective for most businesses as following up with email.

However, it can still be well worth the effort for many businesses, especially when used in combination with the other marketing methods listed in this book. Just remember, to be worth the effort, we need a positive return on our metrics. This metric is likely to be financial return, though you may also be measuring for the reach of your message.

For some industries, social media is a total waste of time. For example, a plumber will most likely waste a lot of time or money if they engage in social media. There are just so many better places to put their marketing energy. (When was the last time you were excited to see what a plumber managed to unblock that day?) Others, such as fashion, can do very well.

To follow up on social media, you first need to get visitors to like you, follow you, link with you, or friend you (depending on the social media platform's terminology of choice). There are several tips to doing this, though most businesses get it incredibly wrong.

It appears the most common approach is to put a stack of social media icons in the site header and then hope for the best. Having a header full of external links is generally not a good idea. The last thing you want is to send visitors into the social media abyss the moment they arrive on your site.

The chances are they won't though, as you have yet to give them any good reason to visit your social media profile. Which leads us to the first tip; put social media links where it makes sense.

For example, Pinterest pins on images, Facebook share links at the bottom of articles, LinkedIn profile links on the about us page etc. Also, put them in the footer and the contact us page for those actively seeking a social media connection, as this is where people typically look.

To make social media work, you need to post at least once a month, but ideally weekly or daily (it will depend on your niche). There is nothing worse than an out-of-date profile. A lack of recent updates creates 'negative social proof', and can lose you sales. Better no social media than bad social media.

Follow Up

The two exceptions to this are LinkedIn and TripAdvisor. However, even these should be kept up to date, and any messages or reviews responded to promptly.

What you post is equally important. People don't care about your constant self-promoting. The trick to making social media work is to post content people care about. And that is where having a purpose-driven business can give you a real advantage, especially when it comes to getting your content shared.

Every business wants their posts to 'go viral', but this seldom happens. Most are lucky to get a single share. However, if you create fun, engaging, and hopefully, meaningful content, you dramatically increase your odds.

When people use social media, they are like an ADHD six-year-old after dessert at a birthday party. Their attention span is barely a few seconds, and they're clicking on anything and everything. Your job is to grab their attention in a sea of visual noise, and hold it long enough to get them to understand the message you're trying to communicate.

To do this create posts that are not only interesting, but also visually engaging with well-written headlines. A general rule of thumb is to keep social media posts short and to the point.

Increasing Revenue

Increasing Revenue

Adding Upsells

An easy way to increase the revenue in many businesses is to offer an upsell. (There is some technical differences with upsells and cross-sells, but for the purposes of this chapter, I will refer to them both as an upsell.)

McDonald's made this strategy famous with their 'would you like fries with that?', a question that has created billions in additional sales. (Or, if you order fries, you will be asked to add a coke, a dessert, or upsize your order.)

When a customer has already taken out their credit card, it is a lot easier to convince them to buy something extra. To get the best result from this strategy, ensure whatever you offer is relevant, and adds additional value to their initial order.

An upsell could be adding an extra warranty, providing VIP support, offering some accessories, suggesting a complementary product, or it could be as simple as the option to upgrade to an overnight courier.

Every business is different, but most can offer something else at checkout. Doing so increases the average transaction value, which, therefore, increases the return on your marketing spend.

You can add an upsell at multiple points during a buying sequence. The best for your business will depend on the product or service and if you are selling online, over the phone, or in person. Here are a few ideas to get you started…

- Have a popup making a recommendation every time someone adds an item to the shopping cart.

- Make a special offer at the point of online checkout.

- Have a 'customer only' limited time special offer after they make a purchase.

- If you take orders over the phone, have a special upsell offer that you present just before taking the customer's credit card.

- If you are selling instore, then have a sign at the counter to promote a discount offer with any purchase.

- Train your staff to make a particular recommendation or offer when processing an order.

Increasing Revenue

Have A Subscription Option

Subscriptions are a great way to create repeat business, which can dramatically increase the lifetime value of a customer. Subscriptions are especially beneficial as you do not have the upfront expense of acquiring a new customer.

There are many ways of adding a recurring payment option, but as with upsells, the best method varies from business to business. Here are a few suggestions to stimulate your creativity...

- If you sell consumables, offer a discount for automatic reordering (very common with supplements but can work with most things that people need to replace continually).

- Service-based businesses (consulting, legal, accounting, window cleaning, beauty, etc.) are perfect for offering discounted rates or a fixed amount of service for a monthly retainer fee.

- If you have high ticket items, offer them on a monthly rental or lease type agreement.

- Have a paid membership with a monthly gift, a member's discount on any purchase, and other special members only benefits.

- Offer VIP support on a monthly contract.

- Offer insurance on products you sell.

As you can see, there are very few businesses that could not find some form of a subscription-based model to generate recurring revenue. The trick to getting people to take up your offer, is to deliver exceptional value and remember to tell your customers about the offer!

Promote Partner Products

Generating additional revenue in your business does not need any investment or cost you much time. By partnering with other non-competitive companies who share your same customer base, you can quickly increase the value of your prospect and customer lists.

Many businesses are more than willing to pay a commission, either for a qualified lead, or for a sale. (Qualified leads are purchased at a low rate, regardless whether they result in a sale or not, sales commissions get paid only if the referral results in an actual sale.)

These commissions are basically free revenue for your business. Once set up, it will keep running indefinitely. You don't need to put any money into stock, you don't need to close a sale, you don't need to deliver anything, and you don't need to provide any support. Just make the referral and get paid your commission.

The only thing you need to do is find the right business to partner with and then set up the referral process. You can automate much of this referral by educating your leads or prospects via your autoresponder and then positioning the business you refer to as a recommended solution. Each time a new person enters your mailing system, an email is sent (at the scheduled time, which may be days or weeks later), and the referral happens on autopilot.

Another way is to include a letter or brochure with products you send out or you give to someone after providing a service.

Do not underestimate this method of generating revenue. Some businesses entire income comes from doing only this.

Affiliate revenue can also be another way for non-profits to create cash flow outside of grants and donations. For every non-profit, there are multiple businesses that can offer something of related value and who would love to donate the commissions from referral sales to a good cause.

The success of this strategy is simply to find the right partners then integrate and automate your referral.

Increasing Revenue

Decrease Customer Cost

Customer Acquisition Cost (CAC) is a fundamental business metric, yet it is a concept few business owners fully understand. Worse, it is one that many never even plan for or build into their pricing.

There are many ways of acquiring a customer; referrals, newspaper ads, Google Ads, radio, SEO, social media, flyers... and each come with a cost; time taken, print costs, ad spend, etc. Now divide this cost by the number of new customers your marketing generates (which will depend on your conversion rates) to give the CAC.

The lower your CAC, the more profit you have in each sale (and if your CAC is higher than your profit margin, you are in trouble). There are several ways to reduce acquisition cost, so let's take a look at some of the most effective...

The first we have already talked about, which is to increase your conversion rate. If you spend $1,000 on ads and get only two sales, your CAC is $500. If you increase your conversion rates to make five sales from the same traffic, your CAC is now just $200.

The second is to stop spending money on leads that don't convert. Preventing this wasted spend is easier said than done, and never a black and white solution. However, with good tracking, you can quickly see what is working well, what produces okay results, and what is just a waste of time. The results are often surprising, with many popular advertising methods delivering poor results.

Of course, if your website is not converting, then all traffic sources will perform poorly, which is why plugging the leaks there should always be the first port of call.

By stopping ineffective ad spend, you improve your CAC and free up some of your marketing budget to test new avenues, or expand those that you can see are working.

The third technique is to increase the number of leads you get for your ad spend. By increasing your ad copy's quality, you increase the number of leads you get for your money. This results in more sales, and, so, lower CAC.

This improvement is true even for most Pay Per Click ads (such as Google Ads)—despite paying per click, the cost is lower for ads with higher click rates.

Another way to reduce CAC from sources such as Google or Facebook Ads, is to optimise the campaign set up. There are many different settings in the various online advertising platforms, and correctly configuring them makes a big difference to your ad spend.

When set up correctly, you will find you benefit from better-quality leads and reduce how much you pay for each click. Both benefits ultimately reduce CAC (and therefore increase profit).

Increasing Revenue

Increase Your Price

A few years back, I was consulting for a guy who was generating leads from Facebook. He was paying for ads that sent traffic to a page offering a blueprint set for $7. This offering was not his main product, but just a way to pre-qualify leads and help build a list.

The trouble was that he was making an average of 80¢ for every dollar he spent. He was quite happy with this, as his real money came from upselling the leads on an advanced training course. Even so, it would have been better if this list building exercise paid for itself.

I suggested putting the price to $9, which he initially resisted, worrying that it would reduce the number of people who took his offer. He decided to run a test on it, and was blown away by the results... the conversion rate actually increased, and he went from losing money to making money on every lead he acquired.

Increasing your price does need to be done with care, but many business owners are just too scared, worrying it will lose them sales. Raising prices is a part of doing business—costs go up, and unless your prices do too, you will reach a point where there is not enough margin to stay in business.

People do shop around for the best price, but the best price does not always mean the cheapest—what they are really looking for is value.

Value is a balance between price, quality, quantity, convenience, and level of service. Look for ways to increase value that allow you to increase your price more than they increase costs.

A business that does not spend money on marketing may never get found. Even if it offered the lowest prices by cutting the marketing cost, few people would ever know to buy.

Remember, in business, we are generally looking for the best return on investment. This return might not always come from getting the highest number of sales. If your margins are meagre, you might make more money by having fewer sales with a higher margin. In other cases, reducing your margins to make more sales may give the best return.

For social enterprises and non-profits, reach may be far more important than profit. If you can make enough to be financially sustainable at a lower price but reach more people, keeping prices low could be a very valid and strategic decision.

Just be careful though—sometimes prices that are too low give the impression of being poor quality and fewer sales than if at a higher price (as with my client mentioned earlier).

If possible, test. By testing different price points and measuring how they affect your conversion rates—and

Increasing Revenue

your bottom line, you can optimise your pricing to get the best result for both you and your customers.

Bonus Tips

Bonus Tips

Create A Quiz

Creating a quiz can be quite a bit of additional work and is a reasonably advanced strategy. However, its many benefits can:

- Grab attention and engage an audience.
- Help your audience feel someone is listening to their personal needs.
- Learn information that allows you to tailor your sales message to your prospects (and so increase conversions)
- Capture and build your list
- Give people something to share on social media
- Help educate people on a topic
- Establish yourself (or your business) as an authority on a particular subject

And many more.

To get the best engagement, make your quiz of value to your audience. To do that, make it relevant and useful. E.g. design it to help answer questions they might have, or build the knowledge on a subject.

At the end of the quiz, ask for their name and email so you can send them the results—and to build your list, of course.

By also sending their answers to your email management system, you can create tags that will allow you to create filters for better follow up.

For example, if someone is interested in small business GST returns, as an accountant, you can follow up with this information, rather than, say; investment advice.

By making the answers to your quiz useful, those taking it will not only be happier they did, but they're also more likely to share it with others. Quizzes can also be a great way to generate qualified leads, increasing your return on the setup cost.

Bonus Tips

Choose Your Platform Carefully

I am consistently saddened by the stream of clients who have received poor advice on which platform to use to build their website. This advice is often by web designers who know little about digital marketing (though unfortunately many pretend to) and simply suggest the system with which they are most familiar.

It is important to remember that your website is not separate from your marketing—it is central to it. The results of many strategies discussed in this book are limited or made possible by the technology used for your website.

This is why we recommend understanding the essentials of digital marketing before you commit to building a website. Understanding marketing allows you to choose a platform that will give you the flexibility to implement the strategies you plan to use.

If you appreciate the importance of CRO, then having granular control over design and split testing will be essential. If you are serious about SEO, you will want a platform that is structured well, and advanced control to optimise settings. If you want to use affiliates to drive your traffic, you will need something that works with an affiliate tracking system.

By choosing a system that can grow over time, you keep your options open and minimise wasted investment. (It sucks to have just paid for a new site, only to find it will not meet your marketing needs.)

Unfortunately, there is no perfect solution. From a marketing perspective, some have far more capability than others. Due to its design flexibility, functionality, and level of control, our personal choice for most projects is WordPress.

By far, it is the most well supported and popular platform, though not without its critics (or issues). The main problems with WordPress all stem from not being set up well. Unlike SquareSpace or Shopify, WordPress needs installing and configuring—and there are almost infinite ways of doing this.

In our experience, the majority of WordPress websites we come across have been poorly built. A badly made site can lead to a system that is ugly, horrible to use, gets hacked easily, runs slowly, and struggles in the search results.

Another challenge with WordPress is to make it work well, you need a variety of premium plugins. These are extensions that help improve all the issues mentioned above, but most come at a yearly cost.

Fortunately, these plugins are usually available with a developer's license, meaning they are much cheaper when you get your website built by a WordPress professional. The same is true for professional hosting. As previously discussed, not all hosting is the same. Hosting optimised for

Bonus Tips

WordPress is far better than the cheap hosting options out there, but it does come at a cost.

Many marketing companies that specialise in using WordPress will offer hosting. Because they get the hosting at a wholesale price, they can often do a better deal than if you try to get the same hosting yourself.

To help overcome a lot of these challenges for our clients, we started *www.EthicalSites.nz*—a WordPress based platform with all the premium plugins included and optimised running on the best servers we could find. EthicalSites includes all the ongoing maintenance, plugin licenses, and support you need. What's more, you can get us to build your site for you, or DIY.

In addition to this, we also offset your site's carbon footprint, plant a tree each month, and protect one thousand square meters of rainforest on your behalf each month. (Since implementing these steps to be more socially responsible, we have not raised pricing, so none of this costs you a cent.)

Check it out at *www.EthicalSites.nz*, and use the coupon code 'ethical-marketing' to get a special reader only discount.

Take An Agile Approach

Many marketing companies create a six month or yearly marketing plan. While these have been the traditional way to approach marketing and can look impressive, they are usually a costly waste.

In recent years, a new, more effective way of doing marketing has evolved. Known as agile marketing, it uses the same underlying principles as agile coding—a programming methodology developed to overcome similar challenges that marketing faces.

The problem is, things change. Predictions about what will work prove wrong. New insights are gained. New ideas are born all the time. New technologies and competitors emerge. Business priorities change. In short, we cannot predict the future well enough to create a plan that is likely to hold up past one to three months, at best.

Agile marketing gives us the freedom to test an idea, measure results, evaluate, and move forward with up-to-date information. Using an agile approach, we may not have a clear plan of the future, but we have a clear strategy for meeting it.

Rather than focusing on a detailed breakdown of what will be done for the next few months, start with the objectives, such as how much revenue you want to increase by over a given time frame, and which other metrics you wish to improve.

Bonus Tips

Next, look at which strategies offer the best return. Is it conversion rate optimisation, starting or improving Google Ads, launching an affiliate program, or focusing on getting found in the search engines? The strategy with the best potential will, of course, depend on your specific business, your budget, your team, and a host of other variables.

The point is, whatever you choose can only ever be an educated guess. Once you begin to implement your strategy, you can use real-world feedback to confirm your decision or adjust it.

There is no point in committing to a marketing approach that is just not working, or missing out on unforeseen opportunities because they did not feature in the original plan.

Do not confuse agile marketing with a free-for-all approach. It has structure, it is just that the structure works with goals that you review periodically and strategies that have short, structured 'sprints' (as opposed to a yearly map).

When a sprint is defined, it maps out what to do over a given time and what that activity hopes to achieve. A sprint may be anything from one week to as much as a month or two, but not longer.

When you create a sprint, goals should be broken down into manageable tasks with realistic timelines and allocated to specific individuals. This way, each task has someone accountable for it, and there is total clarity about what will be done by when.

At the end of a sprint, you and your team can review what actually happened. Were mistakes made, lessons learned, goals achieved? Then you can plan your next sprint accordingly.

The trick to making sprints effective, though, is maintaining discipline. That is, once a sprint has started, see it through without making changes. If you have new ideas, then write them down and save them for the next sprint. If they are now more urgent than all the previous ideas you had, then they can become your new priority.

It is essential to understand that multitasking your team and finances will almost always result in poor results. Sprints allow for a blend of focus and flexibility. All businesses have multiple objectives and limited resources (some a lot more limited than others). Sprints give you a framework to get the best results in the shortest time with the least amount of time or money.

Bonus Tips

Always Be of Service

As we discussed at the beginning of the book, a business is really a form of service to the community. If this becomes central to how you think and operate, then you will enjoy several advantages.

For a start, customers will feel the difference, and they will tell others. We only need to look at our own experiences with other businesses to know this is true. When we experience exceptional service, we tell others. (And, of course, the opposite is also true!)

These word-of-mouth referrals are marketing gold. Never underestimate the value of going above and beyond. It may feel like a short-term loss, but it will pay itself back over time.

More than just pleasing your customers though, when 'being of service' is baked into the DNA of your business, you enjoy your business more. Work becomes more meaningful, as does your life.

In addition, your team will also have greater job satisfaction. This increased satisfaction makes it easier to recruit and retain the people you want to work with, increasing the pleasure of doing business even more.

Creating a service-based mindset and culture in your business may not appear to be an obvious marketing strategy, but it is one well worth implementing.

Get Professional

Perhaps the most common mistake we see businesses making is getting their receptionist, secretary, or family friend who 'knows how to use a computer' to do their website or marketing. Worse, others try to do it themselves.

Having someone unqualified to do your marketing is almost always a bad idea, and is a false economy. I know a good website and marketing can be expensive, but getting them wrong is far more costly. I know, I am biased, but hear me out...

If you are getting a new office built, do you ask your cleaner to build it for you? Even without the legalities, the idea is insane. Just as you would never get surgery from someone who learned how to use scissors in a first aid course or a scalpel in art school.

Yet a large percentage of businesses we come across do precisely this with their website or digital marketing, then wonder why it is not performing as well as they expected.

One of the most common lines we hear is "We just wanted to test it first to see if it was worth investing more into". This is like saying "I will build a wooden shed to see if there is potential for a decent hotel." The only thing you test is whether something built badly will perform badly—and I can tell you the result of that experiment for free.

Bonus Tips

Another mistake is hiring a 'marketing' person as part of the team. You would think this makes sense—after all, they are a professional right? Well, yes and no.

A single marketer is a bit like hiring a Jack of all trades to build your house. They may know enough about everything to get the job done, but don't expect it to be pretty, finished on time, or as good as it could be.

Building a website well requires a range of skills (technical, design, usability, conversions, SEO, etc.), and I have yet to meet anyone who does them all well. Even though I have training and experience in each, I still have a team of experts who specialise in their respective disciplines.

While you may think you are saving money by having someone in-house, more often than not, it ends up costing you far more than it saves (unless you have an in-house marketing team where you have enough full-time work to hire specialists in each discipline).

If someone lacks training, experience, or sufficient time, then chances are, they will not do a good job, which will cost you more in higher ad costs, money wasted on ads that are not working, and lost sales.

There's an exception to this rule: hiring a marketing manager to work with specialised contractors or an agency. This way, they can help develop and implement the big picture while making use of targeted experts.

Ethical Marketing

Trying to save money upfront will usually make getting the job done correctly more expensive. Countless times now, we have had to inform clients that no matter how much they may have spent previously, we need to throw away the existing work and start again.

Staying with the building analogy, imagine starting with some basic foundations... they may be sufficient for a small shack, but you will need to start again at a certain point. It makes no difference how much you paid to get your initial work done; it will be money down the drain.

One of the most common problems we encounter is people not looking into the future. They decide they just want a simple site, then they want to do Google Ads and later SEO. The problem is that often, choices are made early on limit options later (or will end up costing more).

A true professional will sit with you and advise you how to future proof your business. An extra $500 now may easily save you $5,000 down the line. The problem is, many web and marketing agencies try to cut costs to submit the lowest possible price to secure the contract—not good for them or their clients.

If there is one thing to take away from this book, it is that trying to be frugal with web design and marketing is often a dangerous form of false economy. Good marketing makes sales and increases profit.

If you want good marketing, then hire professionals. The extra cost will quickly pay for itself. There is a reason some of the best-paid people in successful businesses are the sales and marketing teams. It is because they get customers—the lifeblood of any business.

I have seen far too many businesses die because the business owner did not value their website or marketing enough to invest adequately into them. The truth is, if a marketing agency is very cheap, it is probably because they don't know how to market themselves or they are hiring staff that are unqualified or inexperienced.

On the opposite side, we have seen many businesses paying far too much. Usually overpaying happens when they don't know how much to expect to pay, what questions to ask, or don't understand the amount of work involved. Hopefully, this book helps you have a more informed conversation with a prospective marketer or designer and increases your chances of making the right choice.

I wish you the best of luck in your endeavours and hope you can use the information in this book to make your business a success and help make the world a better place because of what you do.

Regards,

Leon Jay
Mad Marketing Sage @ EthicallyMAD

About the Author

Leon Jay is an international author and seminar speaker on the topic of online business. He has spoken in the UK, NZ, Australia, America, Thailand, Vietnam, Singapore, China, Indonesia, and Israel.

He has a passion for building businesses and assisting others in their business and marketing strategy. He specialises in seeing opportunity, and identifying false logic or hidden potential.

He started out building a web development business, which he passed on to a business partner to pursue the world of affiliate and information marketing.

Since then, he has served as an affiliate manager for a seven-figure a year personal development company in Australia, and as Director of Marketing at Mark Joyner Inc (Mark is known as the God-father of internet marketing and credited as being the first person to have sold an e-book).

After that, Leon became the marketing mind and 50% partner in a software and training program launch that generated USD1.4 million in 10 days. He has consulted and partnered on various other 6 and 7 figure launches, is founder of *FusionHQ* (a platform for digital and information markers), co-founded *CopySniper* (an online copywriting software and sales page builder), and is co-founder of Coffee Monster (a cafe and co-working space for digital nomads in Chiang Mai Thailand).

In 2012, he was featured on the cover of the Internet Marketing Magazine, a space reserved only for those who have generated more than seven figures online. He has also been featured in several books, and has been a guest speaker on many podcasts and webinars.

After writing his last book, How To Become A Superhero, he founded EthicallyMAD; a project designed to help socially and environmentally sustainable businesses make more of a difference by helping them grow through better marketing and growth hacking strategies.

www.ingramcontent.com/pod-product-compliance
Lightning Source LLC
Chambersburg PA
CBHW071411210526
45465CB00001B/336